THE

# MANUAL TO

# MIDDLE
# SCHOOL

## Books by Jonathan Catherman

*The Manual to Manhood*
*The Manual to Middle School*

THE

# MANUAL TO

# MIDDLE SCHOOL

*The*
## "DO THIS, NOT THAT"
### Survival Guide for Guys

## JONATHAN CATHERMAN
*with*
*Reed Catherman*
*Cole Catherman*

Revell
*a division of Baker Publishing Group*
Grand Rapids, Michigan

© 2017 by Jonathan Catherman

Published by Revell
a division of Baker Publishing Group
P.O. Box 6287, Grand Rapids, MI 49516-6287
www.revellbooks.com

Printed in the United States of America

Library of Congress Cataloging-in-Publication Data is on file at the Library of Congress, Washington, DC.

ISBN 978-0-8007-2847-2

The author is represented by the literary agency of Books & Such.

19  20  21  22  23  24  25          14  13  12  11  10  9  8

# CONTENTS

Introduction: Middle School
     Madness   7

1st Day   10
Absences   12
Announcements   14
Assemblies   16
Backpacks   18
Bathrooms—Keep It Clean   20
Bathrooms—No Loitering   22
Body Odor   24
Book Reports   26
Bragging   28
Brush Your Teeth   30
Bullies   32
Bus—Take Your Seat   34
Bus—Waste Not, Want Not   36
Car Riders   38
Cell Phones   40
Cheating   42
Clothing Style   44
Cologne   46
Communication   48
Crying   50
Cyberbullies   52
Dances   54
Dating   56
Desks   58

Detention   60
Drinks   62
Elective Classes   64
Emotions   66
Face Wash   68
Farting   70
Fights   72
Fire Drills   74
Food   76
Foot Odor   78
Friends   80
Gaming   82
Get to Class on Time   84
Girl Friends   86
Girl's Friends   88
Gossip   90
Grades   92
Grammar   94
Hair   96
Hall Pass   98
Hallways   100
Hand Washing   102
Handwriting   104
Home Room   106
Homeroom   108
Homework   110
Leadership   112
Lockdowns   114

Locker Locks   116
Locker Rooms   118
Lockers   120
Lost and Found   122
Lunch   124
Lunch Line   126
Lying   128
Media Center/Library   130
Money   132
Nail Trimming   134
Name on Your Paper   136
Online   138
Parents   140
PDA   142
Physical Education   144
Pop Quizzes   146
Prepared for Class   148
Principal   150
Problem Solving   152
Puberty   154
Raise Your Hand   156
Reading for Fun   158
Reading for School   160
Report Cards   162
Respect Upperclassmen   164

School Pictures   166
Shaving   168
Showering   170
Siblings   172
Sick Days   174
Skipping School   176
Social Media   178
Sports   180
Stealing   182
Studying   184
Substitute Teachers   186
Swearing   188
Teachers   190
Testing   192
Texting   194
Track the Teacher   196
Trash   198
Voice Changes   200
Voice Volume   202
Writing Papers   204
Yearbook   206
Zombies   208

Riddle Me This   211
Notes   217

# INTRODUCTION

## Middle School Madness

Congratulations, you've made it to middle school! Gone are the elementary days of line leaders, bathroom buddies, and running from girls infected with a sure fatal case of the cooties. Ahead of you are the middle school ways of changing classes, herd-like hallways, lockers, homework, studying, clubs, sports, dances, parties, and yes . . . girls.

Maybe you're one of those guys who thinks he is totally prepared for middle school. Umm, you're not. Could be you're questioning if you even have a snowball's chance in August of surviving. Yeah, you will. No matter how you see yourself right now, it's best to learn this fact. From the dawn of time guys have made it through similar coming-of-age stages in life. This just happens to be your first really big one.

Back in ancient history, guys about your age might have set out into the wilderness on a solo walkabout to prove themselves. Consider this: The original *Survival Man* series was exactly that. Can a young man-in-the-making survive in the wild, kill a beast with sharp teeth, fashion clothes from the hide, carve weapons from the bones, receive some spirit name, and then return home to take a wife? As cool as this may sound, let's face the facts. Most middle school guys today wouldn't last an hour under those conditions. Worse than the danger of death by wild animal, there was no Wi-Fi way back then. The middle school jungle you are about to enter is totally wired and ruled by class schedules, bells, tests, homework, hormones, cliques, jocks, geeks, and a few bullies. As wild as this may sound, survival is pretty much guaranteed. Want proof? It's called high school.

Your family may be saying stuff like "You're growing up so fast" or "Why can't you stay my little boy just a little longer?" They know that's impossible and you don't really want to keep the baby face you had back in elementary school. Nope, you are moving up to middle school, and to be totally truthful, it's not going to be all fun and games. At the same time, you don't want to resist the advancement. If you try to avoid the changes and challenges ahead, you'll hear family and teachers start to say stuff like "It's time to grow up and start taking responsibility for yourself!"

Ready or not, it's best to move into middle school with some good advice from a few good guys. That is what this book is all about. Good advice from good guys who know what they are talking about. How much do they know, you ask? Well, the three guys who wrote this book all made it through middle school alive. All our major organs are still tucked neatly inside our bodies and we graduated up to high school a bit smarter, thanks to our teachers and parents. We wrote this book as a father-son team of middle school survival experts. Reed and Cole have the most recent experience, while Jonathan can say the 8th grade was the best two years of his life. Seriously. You will read more about that fun fact later in the book. To his benefit, Jonathan eventually made it out of middle school and went on to become a bestselling author and a professional sociologist with an expertise in teens, student leadership, and character development.

For now, please accept this book as our gift to you in your middle school years. We believe in you. We hope what you read next will help you be and do your very best in middle school and beyond. Good luck.

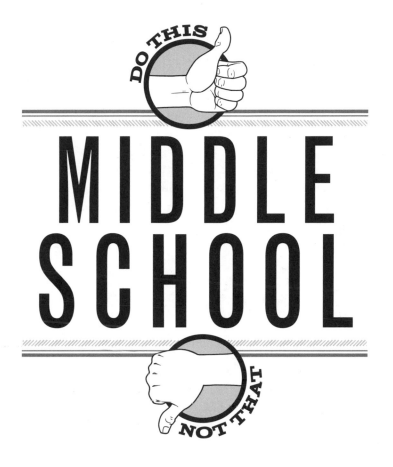

# MIDDLE SCHOOL

# 1st DAY

**B**efore you arrive for the first day of middle school, it's best to know a little about what you're stepping into. Here's what you need to know about the first day. At least one-third of the students are new to the building, and they are feeling about the same as you. The older kids are excited to see their friends, so they won't pay much attention to the newbies walking around. The building is bigger, halls are louder, and passing between classes can be like moving through a crazed herd of cats. The truth is, you might get lost once or twice on the first day of school. But don't worry about it because you won't be the only one. A right turn down the wrong hall can send anybody into the land of the lost. If you do find yourself wandering around, don't freak out. Your best plan for getting back on track and heading the right direction is only three steps away.

> **STEP 1**—Ask for directions. The worst thing you can do is keep standing there looking lost.

> **STEP 2**—Get moving. The classroom isn't coming to you, so don't just stand there.

> **STEP 3**—Don't make excuses. When you do finally make it to class, just tell the teacher that you got lost. They'll totally understand when you're honest about an honest mistake.

## Pop Quiz

**Q:** Where is the school gym?

**A:** You have no idea, so tape a school map on the inside cover of a master folder. When you get lost, just open the folder, read the map, and find your way to gym class.

# ABSENCES

According to experts in every middle school attendance office world-wide, there are three legit reasons to be absent from school:

**Reason #1**, Sick—An infection, affliction, or disorder that can be examined, diagnosed, and verified. Symptoms include a high temperature, migraine, chunks hurling out of either end of your digestive system, broken bones, or another verifiable injury. NOT sick is when you are faking it.

**Reason #2**, Family emergency—Situations calling for immediate action, like the passing of a family member, your home is damaged by a freak weather storm, or the zombie apocalypse. NOT a family emergency is the death of your goldfish, girlfriend breaks up with you, or your favorite jeans didn't get washed due to a false call on that zombie apocalypse thing.

**Reason #3**, Professional intervention—When serious life or legal needs require outside professional or legal help. These may include, but are not limited to, counseling, court, or a doctor appointment. NOT an intervention includes "doing time" on the beach or a 10-hour therapy session with "Dr. Pillow."

When you are absent for a day or two, bring a parent's or doctor's note to the office with an explanation of your absence.

 **Quote**

"Don't pretend to be sick and stay home to get out of a test or project. Fake absences still mean making up class and homework when you come back. There goes all your free time for a couple days."

Cole

# ANNOUNCEMENTS

**E**ach morning a mystic voice from the great beyond will guide you into the school day. Actually, the voice will come from a squawking overhead speaker or live screen broadcast from a "studio" somewhere in the media center or main office. Either way, the info shared over the school announcements is worth paying attention to if knowing today's lunch menu, the bell schedule, the next hat day, or the grade level winning the school-wide penny drive fundraiser is important to you. Such information is power, so sit down, listen up, and collect all the news you need to rule the day.

## True Story

Did you know popular radio personality, television host, and media producer Ryan Seacrest started his broadcasting career doing his school's announcements? "I wore braces and glasses and was fat and got teased about it. But I was always very ambitious."[1] After gaining experience over the morning announcements airwaves, he landed an internship at WSTR Radio in Atlanta, Georgia. Then he was off to study journalism at the University of Georgia before moving to California. The rest is Hollywood magic, and a lot of hard work.

# ASSEMBLIES

The freedom of assembly is an important part of the First Amendment to the United States Constitution. When the Founding Fathers penned the rights of our nation, they stated that the people are allowed peaceful assembly. Never did they imagine packs of savage students swarming in crazed assembly. Pep rallies, awards presentations, talent shows, and guest speakers are all perfect times for the entire school to get together and have some fun. The freedoms students get to experience in assemblies include laughing, learning, clapping, cheering, and being part of stuff like class competitions and fun games. Sleeping, farting, pushing, pranking, and disrupting an assembly are not freedoms, are not protected, and will not be tolerated. So enjoy the break in the school day, keep the gathering peaceful, and the school will grant you the freedom to assemble in another assembly soon.

## To Do in Middle School:

✓ Volunteer to represent your grade in a school assembly class competition.

# BACKPACKS

**M**ost schools allow students to carry some of their books and class supplies in a midsize backpack. This reduces your need to stop by your locker between every class and makes it easier to carry stuff between home and school. Some guys get the wrong idea about how to use their pack and overstuff it like they are on a yearlong wilderness expedition. Other guys rarely clean out their packs. Old food and sweaty gym clothes quickly go rotten, turning your tote into a putrid canvas petri dish. Your best bet is to pack light and keep it clean. Your back muscles—and the nose of the kid walking behind you—will appreciate it.

## Strange but True

Experts recommend a student's backpack should weigh no more than 10–20% of their body weight.[2] Yet on average, 6th graders carry backpacks weighing 18.4 pounds. Incredibly, some student packs weighed in as heavy as 30 pounds! What are they stuffing in there? Is math class meeting on the summit of Mt. Everest?

# BATHROOMS
## KEEP IT CLEAN

**T**here are only two good reasons to visit the room of thrones and neither of them includes trashing the place on purpose! Seriously, do what you have to doo-doo, if you need "two," but keep it clean. Flush from your mind the urge to mark the walls, clog the sink, or scratch the mirrors before returning to class.

**Strange but True**

Most people "visit" the toilet 6 to 8 times a day. That adds up to an average of 2,555 times a year. At about 2 minutes per stop, the total is just over 85 hours a year of bathroom usage. Divide those 85 hours of toilet time by 24 hours in a day and wow! You spend almost 4 full days per year using the toilet.

# BATHROOMS
## NO LOITERING

**W**hen you tinkle, you sprinkle, and while in the stall, don't touch the wall. The truth is there's no escaping germ exposure in the bathroom, public or private. This is bad news for germaphobes and grunge-mongers alike. With every "use," particles of fecal bacteria go airborne and land on the floor, walls, and your hands. It doesn't even matter if you're a "foot flusher," nobody gets away germ free. To make it simple for all to understand, every time you "go," particles of pee and poo stick to you.

The solution is simple. NO LOITERING! Limit your exposure to toxic toilet terrors by not staying and playing in the bathroom. That and always, always, always wash your hands before leaving.

And PLEASE use soap!

### *Just Joking*
**What did one toilet say to the other toilet?**

**You look flushed.**

# BODY ODOR

Imagine raising your hand to ask the teacher for a bathroom pass. Suddenly your nose picks up the foul scent of body odor. In horror you realize the pungent perfume is your personal brand of BO. But it's too late. Before the recoil of your arm can close the pit door, an invisible toxic cloud has escaped into the air.

"Who will smell me?" you ask yourself.

"The cute girl to my right? Please no!" you beg in a silent prayer.

"Maybe nobody will notice," you hope in vain.

But then you hear it. The guy sitting directly behind you fakes an attention-getting gag as he holds his nose and points in your general direction.

*Rewind . . .*

There's no need to sweat it. You can raise your hand high with the sweet smell of confidence if you simply shower daily and apply a few swipes of antiperspirant or deodorant to your clean, dry pits. Who knows whose nose will thank you first—yours or the girl sitting on your right.

## How To . . .
### Apply Deodorant or Antiperspirant

*Preparation—After showering, dry your armpits.*

**STEP 1**—*Remove cap from deodorant.* Peel off any product seal from the stick of antiperspirant or deodorant.

**STEP 2**—*Raise one arm.* Lift your arm over your head to expose your open, dry armpit.

**STEP 3**—*Apply the deodorant.* Swiping up and down in even strokes, apply the deodorant to the skin in your armpit. Repeat under your other arm. Two or three strokes should ensure complete coverage. Too much and people will smell your deodorant before they see you.

**STEP 4**—*Dry time.* Before putting on a shirt, allow a minute for the deodorant to dry so it won't leave a visible mark on your clothing.[3]

# BOOK REPORTS

You are but one guy, writing one paper, in a class of twenty students, all with the same assignment. Your teacher is but one person, grading each paper, from twenty students, all with different perspectives. How will the teacher ever know if you truly read the book? It's just so much easier to skim a few pages, rephrase the book's description, and search the internet for some "ideas" that can be copied, cut, and pasted. Well, believe it or not, teachers know the difference. Maybe it's because they are trained professionals with a degree and official certificate to teach the very class requiring a book report. Maybe it's because they've read way more papers than you'll ever write, and they can smell a false report in the ink. Your best plan is to do the right thing and actually read the book. Think ahead, pace out the pages, take notes, and draft a real report that reflects what you discovered. Who knows? You might just surprise yourself and enjoy the read.

## Looking Back

I wish I had taken more time to reread my work before sending it off to my editors. If I had reread my own writing I could have saved the editors hours of mental pain and myself from countless minor embarrassments.

Jonathan

# BRAGGING

**I**t's not bragging if you actually did it," many guys say proudly.

Yeah, but how many times do you need to tell us you did it? Once is cool. Twice is good. Three times or more and now you're boasting. If you're really that good, then others will talk about you, for you. Try this instead. Be interested in other people's interests and accomplishments first. Then when they feel understood and appreciated, they just might ask you about your accomplishments.

## *Just Joking*

Two guys were busy bragging to each other. The first said, "I can play online all day before my Goldorf Spear is depleted in the Octanian forest."

The second guy replied, "Yeah, my old system used to have really slow download speeds too."

# BRUSH YOUR TEETH

Everybody likes a friendly smile. Go ahead and show us your pearly whites. Your choppers, fangs, chiclets. Most adults have 32 naturally off-white teeth in their mouth. You may still lose a few in middle school, but basically the tusks in your trap are ones you'll want to keep for life. This means brushing your teeth every morning and evening, at least. Brushing *with* toothpaste for about two minutes removes food particles and plaque and helps prevent tartar, gum disease, and halitosis. Hal-i-to-sis is the technical term for bad breath from a dirty mouth. Breathing out of a dirty mouth is also called stank steam, dragon air, yack chat, and the breath-o-death. Failing to brush your teeth produces a smell that will tell the people you are talking with, "No, I didn't fart. I breathed in your general direction." So give your grin a good scrub a few times a day. Your mouth—and noses everywhere—will thank you.

## True OR False?
### The tongue is the strongest muscle in the body.

**False.** The tongue is not just one muscle; it's actually made up of a team of eight separate muscles. This fun fact disqualifies it from all future single-muscle competition. The hardest working muscle in the body is the heart. Yet, fail to scrub your tongue while brushing your teeth, and your death breath might just give somebody a heart attack.

# BULLIES

**B**ullies are like skunks. From far off, they can be avoided. But when one crosses your path, life can really start to stink. So follow your nose and steer clear of the haters. That's all a bully really is, a hater. For some very real reason, they don't like themselves much and are choosing to take their frustrations out on others. Don't be that guy. Instead, be kind to everybody. Even the haters? Yes, even the haters. But when you do find yourself on the stink end of a bully's day, don't freak out and draw attention to yourself. Instead, try to stick with your friends and go immediately to talk with an adult you trust—like a teacher, advisor, or school administrator.

## Ask a Middle School Survivor

**Q:** I just know my older sister's friends are going to pick on me when I'm in middle school. How do I deal with them bullying me at school?

**A:** Sorry to hear about your sister's friends. So, technically bullying is repeated, unwanted, aggressive behavior that involves a real or believed power imbalance. If your concerns become real and they threaten you physically or play mind games with you, then ask your sister to back you up. Family first! If she won't help you out, go over her head and talk to an adult. You can talk with a guidance counselor, teacher, staff person, or parent. Remember, dealing with this kind of stuff is the guidance counselor's job.

Reed

# BUS
## TAKE YOUR SEAT

**I**n kindergarten you learned a simple song that went something like this:

> The wheels on the bus go round and round,
>> round and round,
>> round and round,
> The wheels on the bus go round and round,
>> all through the town!

In middle school you'll want to avoid learning a similar song that goes like this:

> The bus driver's head spins round and round,
>> round and round,
>> round and round,
> The bus driver's head spins round and round,
>> when you don't SIT DOWN . . . and SHUT UP!

Consider the bus a mobile extension of the school. The good behavior your teachers expect of you in class is also expected of you on the bus. So take your seat, face forward, talk quietly, and always be nice to the bus driver.

## True OR False?

**The bus driver has no real authority to discipline misbehaving riders. Basically, what happens on the school bus stays on the school bus.**

**False.** Misbehavior on a school bus can result in suspension of riding privileges, ISS (in-school suspension), and even criminal charges.

# BUS
## WASTE NOT, WANT NOT

The school bus is not a rolling garbage can. Nobody wants to sit on a bus, period. Absolutely nobody wants to ride in a trashed bus littered with crushed wrappers, ripped paper, old gym shoes, and the rumor of a live rodent named Whiskers that's infected with rabies. So keep your trash to yourself. Keep whatever you bring on the bus *off* the floor, and take it with you when you get off the bus.

### *Just Joking*
#### What's the difference between a garbage truck and a school bus?

One makes frequent curbside stops, is crammed with bags, and smells bad. The other is a garbage truck.

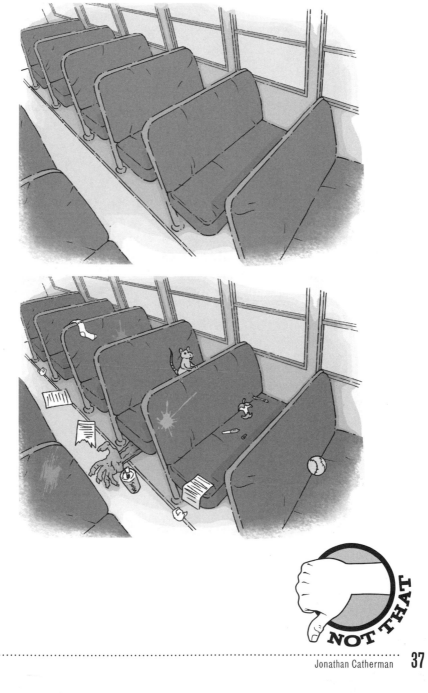

# CAR RIDERS

The school's car rider pickup line shares one thing in common with its southern cousin, the NASCAR pit stop. Both have made a sport out of driving around in circles and only stopping to pick up what's needed before heading back out again. The difference is how long this exchange takes. NASCAR drivers hit the pits at high speed, change four tires, top off the tank, wipe down the grille, and make minor adjustments in about 12 seconds. Whereas the school's car rider line looks more like downtown Los Angeles traffic during rush hour. Parents waiting for students to be released pass the time by snacking, reading, texting, sleeping, and gossiping on social media. Yet both the pro-sponsored drivers and chaffeur-like parents must focus on the same goal. Drive in, pick up, and drive out again safely and as quickly as possible.

So do your part and be ready to go when it's your turn to get picked up. Be safe and be quick about it. This way your afternoon can get back on track as fast as possible.

### Strange but True

On turns, NASCAR drivers can experience 3 G's of force against their bodies. This is the same measure of force that astronauts experience during liftoff.

# CELL PHONES

**T**he major organs you need to maintain a happy and healthy life include the heart, lungs, kidneys, liver, intestines, and a bunch of other very important and equally slippery body parts. Missing from the list of vital parts is what many guys consider a required lifeline to their daily survival—the cell phone. Fail. Contrary to popular belief, lacking access to a mobile device will not send you to the emergency room nor to the top of the tech transplant list. The truth is, when school rules or class codes exclude cell service, you'll survive. Power it off and put it away, before it gets confiscated.

**Strange but True**
In 1983 the first mobile phone in the US cost a mere $4,000.

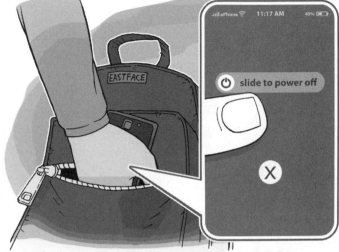

# CHEATING

**C**heating is easy and for the lazy in life. Thinking the teacher is "dumb" and won't catch you doesn't make the teacher the fool. Instead it shines a light on the fact that you have been trusted with far more than is deserved. Instead of sinking low by cheating, hold your head high and try something a bit more challenging. Build your character on the foundation of honesty, truth, and integrity. You'll be stronger, taller, and smarter for it.

 **Quote**

> Dungy, Tony (@tonydungy) "Integrity is what you do when no one is watching; it's doing the right thing all the time, even when it may work to your disadvantage." 18 May 2011, 2:57 PM. Tweet

# CLOTHING STYLE

**S**tand out or blend in—the choice is yours. The style of clothes you choose can make an outward statement of the inward you. Many guys in middle school end up dressing a lot alike, and that's okay. Some guys like the athletic look and will walk the halls with their friends, wearing basically the same stuff, just in different colors. Others will choose a more unique style and try to match their hair color to their blue suede shoes. Some guys will wear gear one day that is different than the way they dressed the day before, and that's okay too. You will see guys wearing everything from sci-fi printed T-shirts to collared dress shirts, trendy necklaces to traditional neckties, jeans to sports shorts. Unless there is a standard uniform all students must wear every day, you can expect to see about every style the school's dress code will allow. So experiment with the looks you like and wear each with pride. Just remember, clothes look best when they are not imprinted with wrinkles, are clean both to the eye and nose, and are respectful of the people and place around you.

## Ask a Middle School Survivor

**Q:** What if I only have one or two pairs of shoes? Is this going to be embarrassing?

**A:** How many pairs of shoes you wear shouldn't be a problem. I know for some guys, their shoes really matter. Still, be sure to keep the ones you have clean and aired out. What's embarrassing is to walk around with dirty, smelly shoes with the laces untied. Also, smile a lot and people will keep looking up at your face instead of down at your shoes.

Cole

# COLOGNE

**H**ate to break it to you, man, but cologne is really just perfume for guys. First called cologne by the perfume mixologist who concocted it way back in 1706 while working in a little German town called, wait for it . . . Cologne, the name and manly smell have both stuck around. Today all guy perfumes hold the same generic title. Perfume has been lingering a bit longer, dating way, way back to the second millennium BC. The name comes from a Latin word literally meaning "through smoke," which is what you are going to avoid when wearing your selection of *through smoke*. Cologne is supposed to be applied in small amounts. Never are you to splash or spray a smoldering, thick cloud of the stuff on yourself, your clothes, or anybody else. The cologne you wear was not brewed to cover your BO, advertise your arrival, or loiter in the air long after you walk by. Wear it wisely and only occasionally, if you wear it at all.

## How To . . .
### Apply Cologne

**STEP 1**—Pick one scent. Don't mix scented body wash, deodorant, and hair products in the same air as your cologne.

**STEP 2**—Remove cap. Point away from your eyes when doing so.

**STEP 3**—Apply cologne. Spray or dab a light amount to the skin on the base of your neck. Never apply to fabric, as the smell will change and stains can occur.

**STEP 4**—Recap cologne. You don't want to spill the stuff.

# COMMUNICATION

**C**ommunication is a numbers game, and you want to win this game. To win, you'll need to do some math. Don't freak out. It's easy. To communicate your way to a win with teachers, coaches, and your parents, do the math so your communication equals 100%:

55% body language = Face people, look them in the eye, and smile.

38% tone of voice = Speak clearly and be respectful—no sarcasm.

7% words = Choose your words carefully and stay away from extreme descriptions like "always" or "never," "everybody" and "nobody."

## How To ...
### Show You Are Listening in Class

**Sit up.** Sitting up communicates that you're alert and engaged.

**Listen up.** Listening to your teacher and other students is a good way to make them feel like what they have to say is important.

**Ask questions.** Teachers like it when you ask questions. The trick is to know the right kind of questions to ask:

- **Rule #1**—Ask good questions and expect good answers.
- **Rule #2**—Ask lame questions and you'll get lame answers. (FYI . . . lame questions are intended to distract, disturb, and force the teacher off topic.)
- **Rule #3**—Ask no questions and you'll get no answers.

**Nod your head.** Teachers are really good at reading nonverbal communication. By nodding your head, it lets them know you are getting what they are teaching.

**Track the teacher.** To track your teacher means that when they move from one side of the classroom to the other, you keep watching them as they teach. (See "Track the Teacher.")

# CRYING

**C**rying in middle school is an emotional subject. Some people say guys need to bottle up their feelings. Others recommend just letting it all out. What's clear is the average guy sheds tears about 1.3 times a month. These tears range from "No, I'm not crying. I've just got something in my eye" to full-on "get that man a tissue" sobbing. One guy might cry because he just compound-broke like 150 bones in a parkour, major-league, pro-swag move gone terribly wrong. Another will cry from embarrassment when his buddy uploads the video to YouTube and tags it with "EPIC FAIL over the handrail."

If and when you do cry is up to you, yet keep this thought in mind: Gone are the elementary school days of tears over spilled milk or broken pencils. The middle school rules are simple. If you didn't get your homework done, there's no crying. If you forgot the field trip permission slip again, there's no crying. If it's the last day before your best friend moves across the country, it's okay to get a bit teary-eyed. If you just learned your parents are splitting up, go ahead and open up. If you do feel like a cry is about to happen at school, go talk with your class advisor or school counselor. They'll work to assist you through whatever you're wrestling with, and for sure they can spare a tissue or two.

## True OR False?

### Crocodiles really do shed tears.

**True.** For a long time, insincere people have been said to cry "crocodile tears." Now researchers have found some reptiles really do shed tears. The reason is most likely biological rather than emotional.[4]

# CYBERBULLIES

**A**lmost everybody is digitally connected today. Wired or wireless, a streaming virtual feed of data is available anytime, from anywhere, between anyone. This means flesh-and-bone bullies can make the leap to cyber cruelty with a simple click or post. Like a virus, digital bullies attack with a text, pic, or tag. They rain down the hurt from the cloud of pain in their life. Selfishly, they are trying to raise themselves up by putting others down with posts or texts about something hurtful, mean, or divisive, or something they think is "funny." To keep digital bullies from "caching" in on your story, do your best to follow these digital life do's and don'ts:

1. Do be careful who you friend, follow, and like online.
2. Don't believe everything you find online.
3. Do screen capture when a bully strikes and share the evidence with a trusted adult like a parent, teacher, youth group leader, or school administrator.
4. Don't reply or retaliate to offensive messages.
5. Do be filled with integrity and always guard both your digital and analog life.

## True OR False?

### Life online isn't the same as real life, so digital bullying isn't the same as physical bullying.

**False.** Cyberbullying is real and very illegal. Online bullies can face arrest and prosecution because all 50 states have bullying laws that include harassment by electronic means that threatens another person's physical well-being.[5] The nation-wide trend is toward greater accountability for bullying in general, both in school and off campus. Middle school students have been arrested for cyberbullying and charged with harassment, felony aggravated stalking, and even an offense against a computer system for unauthorized access, which is a felony.

# DANCES

No less than two dozen recording artists have released songs titled "Dance Like Nobody's Watching." That's some solid lyrical advice, considering most middle school guys don't know how to dance well enough to make anybody want to watch. Then there's that one guy who practices at home. When he makes his move to the dance floor, everybody gathers around and cheers. We all love/hate that guy. If you can dance like magic or know your moves are nothing but tragic, it doesn't change the fact that school dances are really all about having fun with your friends. Those chairs along the wall don't need you to hold them down. So don't sit around doing gravity's job. Instead, get up, get out there, and get dancing. Throw your hands in the air and wave 'em like you just don't care . . . like nobody's watching.

## True Story

In the 8th grade I liked the coolest girl in school. She was smart, athletic, pretty, and always surrounded by popular guys with bigger muscles than mine. My only advantage was I owned a pair of parachute pants before any other guy in school. The pants were made of parachute-like material and featured multiple zippers on the legs for an extra edgy look.

I wore the parachute pants to the last dance of the school year. As the final song played, I took a chance and asked the cool girl to dance. She said yes. It was a slow song about a guy dancing cheek to cheek with a lady in red. And there we danced, like the song was written for us, I in my parachute pants and she in a red dress. I knew this was the start of something special. Suddenly the gym lights turned on, she ran over to her friends, I stood there alone, and the moment was lost. Later she signed my yearbook, "You're a really neat guy. See you next year!" Not a word about my parachute pants.

Jonathan

# DATING

**T**he day is near when you'll want to spend some special time with a special someone you think is kind of special. *Wink, wink,* say no more. Actually, there's a lot more to say. Also known as dating, the act of spending time together to learn if you like them and if they like you is totally worth saying more about. Now that you are middle school minded, think about this. What is dating? What isn't dating?

Let's start with what isn't. Acting silly to get attention isn't dating. That's called flirting. Staring from across the cafeteria isn't dating. That's called creepy. Going out of your way to walk by their locker between every class, following them home, and texting messages that took an hour to thumb peck isn't dating. That's called stalking. Don't be a creepy stalker. Dating is when both of you agree that you are going to get to know each other better, slowly. Seriously, there is no need to rush into things socially, emotionally, or physically. Socially, you don't need to make a big announcement to all your friends, in person or online. Emotionally, if you are going to use the "L" word, choose "like" and not "love" till you are way past middle school. Physically, only go as far as you would if your parents were watching. This may all sound weird, and if it does, don't worry about dating until it doesn't.

## True OR False
### Dates and figs are the same thing.

**False.** Figs and dates are two different types of fruits. Fig plants are shrubs, while dates are grown on trees.

# DESKS

**F**ront row or back corner? Beside the window for direct sun, or close to the door for a quick getaway? By yourself for better concentration, or by your friends for more conversations? There are so many choices for where you can sit in class, you might not be able to stand yourself! But before your head gets lost in the cloud of options, keep your feet on the ground and this in your mind. One teacher may give you free-range pickings for where to rest your rear, yet in your next class the teacher could assign your behind to a seating chart. One thing is certain—all desks are "public property." The class before you and the one following have other kids sitting in the same seat. So respect the desk and keep the row straight, circle curved, or group together. Always try to leave your desk as good as, if not better than, the way you found it.

## Quote

"On the first day of school, you got to be real careful where you sit. You walk into the classroom and just plunk your stuff down on any old desk, and the next thing you know the teacher is saying, 'I hope you all like where you're sitting, because these are your permanent seats.'"[6]

—Jeff Kinney, author of the Diary of a Wimpy Kid series

# DETENTION

It seems like everybody gets in trouble at school at least once. Trouble can range from something little, like forgetting to turn in homework and getting a bad grade on an assignment, to something serious that earns the discipline of detention. Google search the "meaning of detention," and the quick search results include the definition "the action of detaining someone . . . in official custody, especially as a political prisoner." Now STOP! Before you go and turn into a middle school student-rights activist, slow your roll and think for a minute. Consider that in the definition of the word *discipline* there is both the positive value of *knowledge* and negative action of *punishment*. Both are options. When you possess the positive value of self-discipline, you are more likely to do the right thing and not get disciplined with detention. Lack self-discipline, do the wrong thing, get in trouble, and be disciplined with detention. Basically you can have discipline and no detention or no discipline and get detention. The choice is yours. If you do find yourself *detained in official custody*, remember this wise advice from a seasoned 8th grader: Figure out what works, and do it as often as you can. Figure out what doesn't work, and stop doing it. That should keep you from getting in trouble more than once.

## Ask a Middle School Survivor

**Q:** What does ISS and OSS mean?

**A:** ISS stands for In-School Suspension. This means you stay at school, do some work around the school, and get your schoolwork done. OSS is Out-of-School Suspension. You can't come back to school till they say it's okay, and getting your schoolwork done is much more difficult without the help of teachers.

Reed

# DRINKS

**T**hirsty much? Hope so, considering 60% of your body weight is water. Getting the wet stuff in is good for flushing out toxins from your body systems and carrying nutrients to your cells. Staying hydrated also helps keep your breath fresh and skin from getting too oily. A good goal is to drink about eight 8-ounce glasses of fluid a day. Everyone's body is dependent on fluids, yet few guys drink as much as they need. Some even say they don't like the naturally tasteless taste of water and prefer slurping down their fluids from an industrial-sized can of chemically sweetened carbonated water. Your preference for pure $H_2O$ or $H_2CO_3$ mixed with natural and artificial flavors is between you and your dentist. What you need to know about drinking water or soda at school is teachers, coaches, janitors, lunch ladies, bus drivers, and carpool parents all hate it when you spill. They're also not big fans of students leaving half-full drinks sitting around for somebody else to "accidentally" kick the can over. It's a good idea to check with your teacher/coach/driver about their beverage policy before you open a can of Get in Trouble at School.

## Looking Back

I'm really glad I got my own reusable water bottle. I filled it each morning with ice and water to drink at school. If I needed to refill it at school, I'd pick my favorite drinking fountain and top it off. Once I got home I'd fill it up again. I recommend a 24-ounce bottle that is dishwasher safe.

Reed

# ELECTIVE CLASSES

**S**ome classes you are required to take. Some classes you choose to take. Many of the core courses like math, language arts, science, and history are all required learning. Elective classes like drama, robotics, band, and computer programming are open for your choosing. The trick is being proactive and thinking ahead while planning your school schedule to include both your required and chosen classes. The good news is, most of the class scheduling process is decided for you each year. Yet within your schedule are one or two class openings where you can "Insert elective course here." But choose wisely, young padawan. Once you have committed to an elective class, it can be difficult to near impossible to change your schedule. So, if Underwater Basket Weaving sounded cool when you signed up for it, but now Advanced Robotics is looking way better . . . it's too late, my waterlogged friend.

## To Do in Middle School:

✔ Go on a class trip. Most grade levels plan a class trip at least once a year. It may be somewhere local, historical, or just for fun. Sometimes a class trip may even be an overnight adventure. Whatever the trip, be sure to get the most out of the opportunity. Have fun, learn some cool stuff, and try to make a new friend along the way.

# EMOTIONS

**E**ver ridden a roller coaster? All those ups and downs, twists and turns, spins and death-defying drops can make a guy feel nervous, scared, and excited all at the same time. That's a lot like the emotional roller coaster known as middle school. One moment you're feeling up, and then down. One day it's "the best of your life" and the next "the worst ever!" Why so many emotional twists and turns? Because middle school is life's prime time for no two days to be the same socially, emotionally, or physically. This can push you toward feelings of excitement and terror all wrapped up in one. But don't worry, it's pretty normal and will eventually smooth out in a turn or two if you do your part to stay on track.

For instance, when your emotions drop, it's not a good time to fly off the rails and experiment with cursing your way through "expressing" yourself. Nobody likes a dirty mouth. Choose your descriptive words carefully and try to stick with "I" language like, "I feel frustrated right now." Stay away from the emotional whiplash that follows blaming others for how you feel, with statements like, "You are so frustrating!" They'll probably get defensive and say something back like, "No, I'm not. You are!" and there you go again—up and down, round and round on the vomit comet of emotional twists and turns. Instead, go for a smoother ride by sticking with "I" language and avoiding the roller coaster run of "you" language. When your emotions do get crazy, and they will, take a minute to chill out and remember that you are in control of you. Stay centered and focus on the positive.

## Pop Quiz

**Q:** Which is the best emoji face to use when breaking up with a "girlfriend" in a text message?

**A:** Trick question! Never break up in a text message. Man up and talk with the girl face-to-face.

# FACE WASH

Let's just face the facts. The zombie apocalypse will never happen, but a true zit invasion is headed your way. So stop obsessing over neutralizing a fictitious herd of grunting corpses and start planning how to defend your face from a puberty-planned pimple occupation. When it comes to fighting the effects of oily skin and acne, your best defense is a good offense. Start your day by washing your face in the shower. Wash again before bonding with your bed at night. Always use a clean washcloth, face soap, and warm water.

## How To . . .
### Wash Your Face

STEP 1—Make it routine. Wash every day, morning and evening.

STEP 2—Wet a clean washcloth with warm water.

STEP 3—Hold the warm washcloth to your face and neck for a minute. This loosens dirt and opens your pores.

STEP 4—Apply mild soap to your face and neck. A nonirritating and alcohol-free skin product works best. (You can buy this kind of skin cleanser at most grocery stores or pharmacies. Ask your parent or a store clerk for help picking one that will work for you.)

STEP 5—Rinse your skin. Use warm water.

STEP 6—Don't touch! Your hands are covered in bacteria, and bacteria love to make zits on your face.

STEP 7—Eat and drink better. Avoid greasy foods high in saturated fat, sugar, and salt. Drink lots of water.

# FARTING

**Y**ou are a walking science experiment that could blow up at any moment. Everywhere you go in school, a strange brew of noxious gasses ferments within you. Those bubbles building in your large intestine are produced "naturally" as your digestive system breaks down breakfast or lunch. The bloated feeling in your belly is nitrogen, hydrogen, carbon dioxide, and methane, which are all odorless gasses. If you are lucky, they might creep out undetected by the average nose. But mix in even a small amount of hydrogen sulfide or ammonia and your roux smells like . . . PEW! Was that you? Not if you pass on passing gas in class. Do the right thing and keep the air clean until you are outside. But when the pressure builds and you just can't hold it in any longer, please let it out in the bathroom.

## *Just Joking*

A boy comes home from school and proudly announces to his parents, "Mom and Dad! The teacher asked the class a question today and I was the only one who knew the right answer!"

The parents are very happy and say, "That's amazing! What was the question?"

Standing tall with pride, the boy says, "Who farted?"

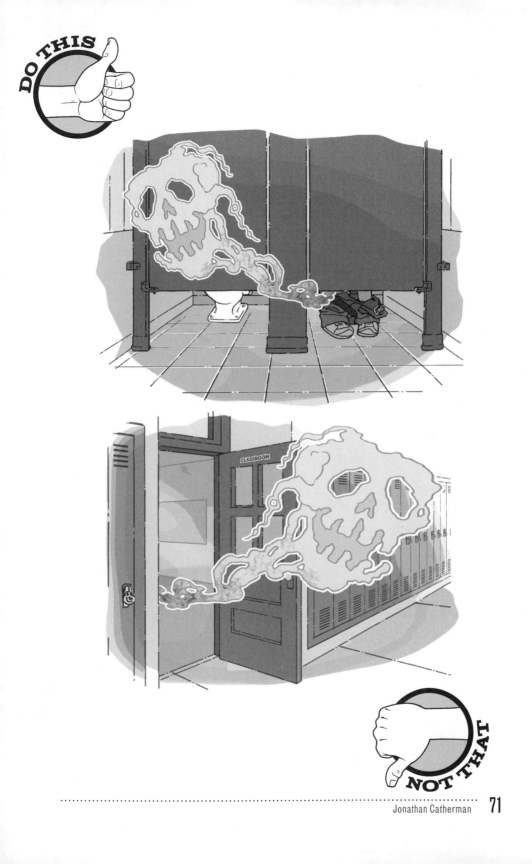

# FIGHTS

**I**t's like some guys are looking for a fight. Maybe they are selfish bullies or were just raised by angry wolves deep in a haunted forest. Whatever the reason for their thin skin and rush to "fighting words," there is no need to meet them in a fist-to-fist brawl. Instead show you are a true tough guy by being in total control of yourself. Be quick to listen, slow to speak, slow to become angry, and the first to use your brain by turning and walking away. Instead of raising their fists, smart guys win battles with their wits. Not only is this a clever way to win, it also avoids the pain that comes with a potential bloody nose, bruised ego, and suspension trip to the principal's office. Remember the wise words attributed to the always great Chuck Norris: "Men are like steel. When they lose their temper, they lose their worth."[7]

## *Just Joking*

- Chuck Norris doesn't drive cars, he flies trains.
- Chuck Norris can speak French . . . in Russian.
- A bulletproof vest wears Chuck Norris for protection.
- Death once had a near–Chuck Norris experience.
- Chuck Norris doesn't dial the wrong number, you pick up the wrong phone.
- When Chuck Norris enters a room, he doesn't turn the lights on, he turns the dark off.
- When a zombie apocalypse starts, Chuck Norris won't try to survive. The zombies will.
- Chuck Norris counted to infinity. Twice.
- When Chuck Norris was in middle school, his English teacher assigned an essay, "What is courage?" He received an A+ for turning in a blank page with only his name at the top.

# FIRE DRILLS

**Y**ou know the drill. When wall-mounted sirens screech loud enough to make your ears want to bleed and mini strobe lights burn blue spots into your retina, it's a fire drill. The school is not actually about to be blown sky-high, yet . . . if a Bunsen burner had tipped over in science class and ignited the hoodie you left dangerously close to an open flame, everybody would know how to get out of the building quickly and safely. But that's not the case today, so all you need to do is remember what you practiced back in the days of elementary school evacuations. Simply follow the teacher's instructions to make your way to the nearest fire-free zone. After a quick head count and the "all clear" is announced, you'll head back to class.

Do know that this is not the time to pull your own version of a Stop, Drop, and Roll drill in the hall. Nor is it your opportunity to fake spontaneous combustion while yelling, "I'm so hot there's no saving me now!" Such behavior is not very bright and guaranteed to make smoke blast out of your principal's ears while burning any chance you have of getting back on your science teacher's good side. Your best bet is to stay cool and calm, and cooperate through the entire drill. That and remember to move your hoodie off the counter when you get back to class.

## Pop Quiz

**Q:** What three things are needed to make fire burn?
   (A) match, candle, cake
   (B) fuel, oxygen, heat
   (C) wood, marshmallow, tent

**A:** (B) fuel, oxygen, heat

# FOOD

**H**ealth class teachers are guaranteed to say some funny stuff like, "You are what you eat, from your head down to your feet." Good thing this is not literally true. If such a statement were factual, most guys would look like a box of pepperoni pizza soaked in an over-caffeinated energy drink. Yet, what goes in must come out, and this happens in both obvious and obnoxious ways. The kind of food you eat and how much you stuff into your face have a direct effect on the quality of your life. The chow you chew powers your daily energy level, brain focus, smell of your breath, stank of your gas, the size jeans you wear, and even the power of your pimples. Basically, food is fuel. Do your best to eat healthy, avoid junk snacks, drink lots of water, and limit the number of pizza slices you send down to stomach storage to less than an attempt on a world record.

## To Do in Middle School:

✓ Volunteer at a food bank to support the work they are doing to supply food and grocery items to people in need.

# FOOT ODOR

**O**kay, daydream about this for a minute. Imagine you are the first human to meet a tiny space alien whose ship crashed in your backyard. The extraterrestrial is peaceful and obviously really smart because his head is huge (for a tiny alien). The little guy likes you so much, our government makes you the alien's teacher about earth's human stuff and a spy about space's alien stuff. All is good until your lessons about earthlings include how our noses run and feet smell. In an attempt to help the confused alien understand the difference between runny noses and smelly feet, you offer the foreigner your shoe and a tissue. With only one sniff of your sneaker, the mini-Martian's skin turns from a cool blue to puke gray. He gasps for air, his nose implodes, and he chokes to death. To make a bad situation even worse, you learn the tiny alien is the royal son of the tiny alien king with an even bigger head. This means you just killed the petite prince with your rank, stank toe jam. The alien king believes you just assassinated his son. He declares war on the third rock from the sun and prepares to hyper jump his Dreadnought Warships into a battle-ready earth orbit. Who knew your foul foot funk could bring about the end of the world!

Well . . . just about every human being has smelled stinky feet and knows the feeling of total doom. So how can you fight off an imaginary alien invasion and avoid the real-life embarrassment of walking around school with smelly feet? Start with washing your feet with soap . . . EVERY DAY! Next, dry your toes before putting on clean socks. Finally, air out your shoes at the end of the day and buy a pair of odor-eating insoles if you need to. These simple actions can save both your reputation at school and the earth from total annihilation.

## Strange but True
Did you know that each of your feet contains a whopping 250,000 sweat glands and can produce a full pint of perspiration per day, per foot? That's a lot of shoe-dew.

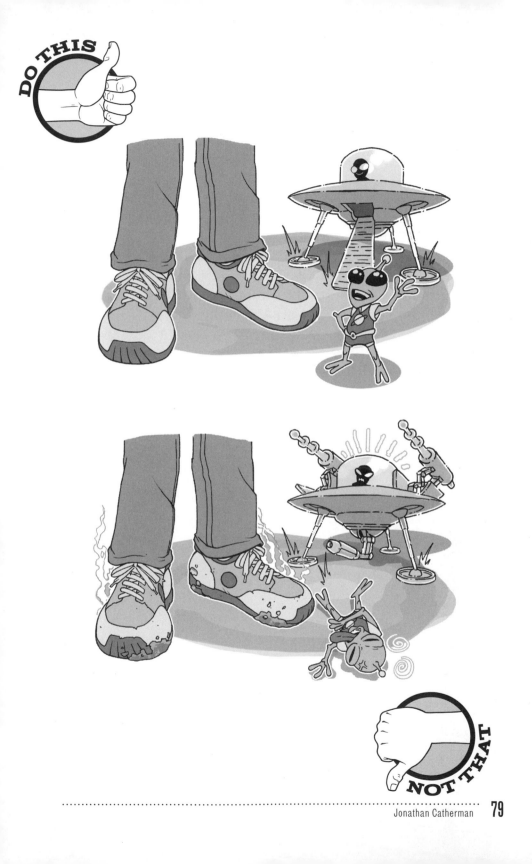

# FRIENDS

**E**verybody needs a few true friends. Some say the number of truly great friends a guy will have in his life can be counted on one hand. This is because there's a big difference between friends who will be there for you through thick and thin and virtual "friends" you collect after an attention-grabbing status post. Your crew, squad, and brothers truly know you and you know them. The best of friends are the ones who make you laugh, inspire you to think about new stuff, challenge you to do cool stuff, and are always there to lift you up. They encourage you to succeed, and when you do, they won't take advantage of you or the situation. Choose your friends carefully, because you will be known by the ones you keep. This may mean you'll need to walk away from "friends" who are a bad influence. Most important, always be the kind of friend you'd like to befriend you.

 **Quote**

"I'm a success today because I had a friend who believed in me and I didn't have the heart to let him down."[8]

—Abraham Lincoln

# GAMING

**R**eality is for losers who don't play video games—unless you are playing in virtual reality, and then you won't believe how actual the game graphics have become," says the gamer totally disconnected from reality. Don't be that guy. Sure, gaming can be a cool part of middle school and beyond. So is being a high score holder in the reality game called life. Discovering the cheat codes to first-person interactions with family, teachers, friends, and other humanoids employs "reusable" hacks that work over and over again, just like in your favorite free roam or sandbox game. To keep your real-world FPS rate smooth, commit the time and attention needed to mastering the game of life just as you would to the latest and greatest digital download. For sure the realities awaiting you outside the game are just as challenging and way more immediate than your call to duty as an alien-killing mercenary.

## True OR False

### The first video game was invented in 1971.

**False.** Physicist William Higinbotham created the first video game in October 1958. It was a very simple tennis game, similar to the classic 1970s video game Pong, and it was quite a hit at a Brookhaven National Laboratory open house.

# GET TO CLASS ON TIME

**G**etting to class on time is not as difficult as you may think. To prove the point, consider the following challenge. Brad and Nick are in the same history class. The bell rings and they leave for their next class at the same time. Their goal is to Beat the Bell and get there in five minutes or less.

—Brad knows what he's doing. He first stops at his locker. Then he walks over to say hi to a friend. Next he makes a quick run to the bathroom, a stop at the trash can, and then straight to his next class. Total time 3:55.

—Nick chooses his own route. First, he goes to the bathroom, then to his locker. After stashing his history book in the locker, he runs outside into the courtyard to yell "hi" to his friends. He rushes back inside and runs the full length of the hall and back again. He drops his backpack on the floor and tries to jump over a trash can. Epic fail. Garbage and Nick spill everywhere. Acting like he didn't do it and nobody saw him, Nick forgets where he dropped his backpack and searches the hall to find it. He stops to get a drink of water just as the bell rings. Nick runs around the corner toward his next class. Total time 5:27. He's late . . . also known as tardy.

The moral of the story? To get to class on time—be a Brad, not a Nick.

### Ask a Middle School Survivor

**Q:** Is tardy just getting to class or being in my seat by the bell?

**A:** Some teachers will count you tardy if you are not in class by the time the bell rings. Other teachers will count you tardy if you are not sitting in your desk by the time the bell rings. It's your responsibility to learn what each teacher means by "tardy."

Reed

SCHOOL MAP

SCHOOL MAP

# GIRL FRIENDS

**I**f all the students in your middle school were to gather in the gym, about half of the kids would be boys and half would be girls. Some of the guys standing around might still think girls are weak, wordy, and wicked, and it's weird to be friends with them. Really, guys? Are we still in the 3rd grade here? Spoiler alert: cooties aren't real and having a friend who's a girl doesn't make her your girlfriend. Friends become friends because they like the same stuff, do the same things, and can trust each other. Guys like sports. Girls like sports. Guys like video games. Girls like video games. Guys like food. Girls like food. Guys like movies. Girls like movies. This means your opportunity to make friends in middle school can and should be a good mix of both guys and girls.

### Ask a Middle School Survivor

**Q:** How do I make friends with a girl without her thinking I like her?

**A:** Just be yourself. Don't flirt with her if you just want to be friends. If you can do these two things, she will always have your back. That's what friends do.

Reed

# GIRL'S FRIENDS

**G**irls are friends with their girl friends in very different ways than guys are friends with their guy friends. Girls create friend titles like "besties" and "BFF" while posting pictures of their hands held together in the shape of a shared heart. Yeah, most guys don't do that. Girls will text their bestie nonstop while sitting right next to each other. Yeah, most guys don't do that either. What a girl shares with her girl friends includes, well, pretty much everything. They share clothes, makeup, headphones, and secrets in ways most guys don't easily understand. Here's an example. Some girls will say to you, "You can tell me. I won't tell anybody." Now, when she says "anybody," that doesn't necessarily mean her BFF won't find out. This is because her BFF isn't just "anybody." A best friend forever is such a close friend, it's like the two are the same as one person. So what you tell one friend, the other is likely to find out. Understand it or not, now you know.

## Strange but True

BFF is the airport code for Western Nebraska Regional Airport, as well as an acronym for an Australian Brush Fire Fighter and the British Fighting Force.

# GOSSIP

**T**he average human mouth can open wide enough to fit three fingers in between the upper and lower front teeth. That is, unless the words spilling from your mouth are gossip vomit, and then an entire foot may easily slip into the same space. "Foot in mouth" . . . what? It's just a saying, yet the meaning is time tested. You see, way back in the 1870s, foot-and-mouth disease was all the rage with cattle. This was a problem and usually meant the cow was foul. The expression "putting one's foot in one's mouth" began to be used as a metaphor for foul people who got in trouble for what they said. Sharing selfish secrets, half truths, and hurtful gossiping got them in trouble then, just as it does today.

Here are two rules you can use to avoid putting your foot in your mouth:

**Rule #1**—If you have a problem with somebody, try talking *with* them rather than about them.

**Rule #2**—Talk about others the way you want them to talk about you.

If somebody is saying gossipy stuff about you, refer back to Rule #1 and ask a trusted adult to go with you to talk with them.

 **Quote**

"As the unknown sage puts it, 'The best minds discuss ideas; the second ranking talks about things; while the third and lowest mentality— starved for ideas—gossips about people.'" [9]

—Admiral Hyman G. Rickover, US Navy

# GRADES

**B**reaking news. Teachers don't "give" grades to students. Instead, students must "earn" their grades. Seriously, you've got to wrap your head around this one. In middle school you must do your part to pick up what the teacher is laying down. It doesn't matter whether or not you like the subject or teacher. Maybe you don't like the teacher's "style." Maybe you don't like the kids in your class. Do or don't, welcome to the big show. Middle school is all about you owning the effort you put into school to get the grades you need to succeed. For some guys school comes easy. They still have to own their goal of getting straight A's in every class. Other guys will have a more difficult time in school. They too must do everything in their power to make a grade that passes them through their courses. Here are a few sure-to-work ways to start owning earning your grades.

1. Come to class, on time.
2. Listen to the teacher.
3. Get organized.
4. Take notes.
5. Ask questions.
6. Don't distract other students or the teacher.
7. Be nice to the teacher.
8. Write your name on your assignments.
9. Do the work and TURN IT IN.
10. Do any and all extra-credit work.

## How To...
### Get Maximum Credit on COMPLETED Classwork

**STEP 1**—Put your name on the top of the page.

**STEP 2**—Turn it in on time.

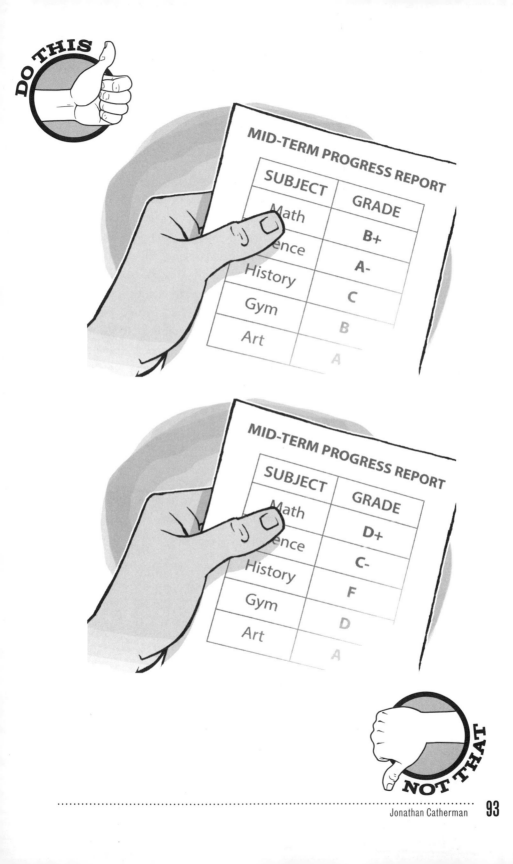

# GRAMMAR

**N**ot long ago High English was the way people who wanted to sound smart talked. Slang-free and always proper, they spoke and wrote in a formal style that showed they knew the language of the educated class. Times have changed and so has the way people write and speak. In the world of a modern middle schooler, texting, messaging, and typing that is automatically spell-checked, auto filled, and abbreviated is perfectly normal. Similarly, the way some people speak has come to include verbal fuzz, mumbling, abbreviations, and slang that may or may not be understood by a teacher, coach, parent, and other students. Said simply, poor grammar can lead to a wealth of confusion. Avoid the confusion and show people just how smart you are by practicing two simple rules of good grammar.

> **Rule #1**—Speak up. You have a wonderful voice, so speak with the clear confidence people need to hear and understand you.

> **Rule #2**—Write well. Teachers don't accept text message abbreviations in sentences, so spell out every word, using every letter.

When you speak and write well, people are more likely to understand, recognize, and respect you as a member of today's educated class.

---

## Pop Quiz

**1.** What is the shortest sentence in the English language?

**2.** More English words begin with this letter than any other letter of the alphabet.

**3.** What is the longest English word that can be spelled without repeating any letters?

**A:** 1. "I am."  2. The letter *S*  3. uncopyrightable

# HAIR

**M**iddle school is filled with unexpected challenges and more than a few frustrations. Finding a hairstyle that works shouldn't add stress to your life. Yet for some guys it does. Either they don't care that their head looks like a dirty mop, or they spend more time than Miss America directing each and every follicle into sculpted perfection. Don't be either of those guys. Instead, work your style until you find a 'do that works for you. Don't be afraid to try a few different looks before deciding on what rests best on your head. Next, find a barber or stylist who knows how to cut your hair the way you like, and stick with them. After that, use good hair products to keep your style looking right. And please, for the sake of the noses that surround you in class, never, never, ever apply fragrance-scented hair gels, pastes, sprays, or other trendy smelling goo to your 'do.

## Strange but True

Hair is strong. A single strand can hold 100 grams or 3 ounces in weight, but combined, the hair of a whole head can hold 12 tons, or the weight of two elephants.[10]

# HALL PASS

To travel freely over borders and between countries in the world requires you to carry a valid passport. To freely move around the school when you should be in class requires an official hall pass. Guarded like government-issued official travel documents, most teachers don't just hand out hall passes to anybody who asks. You'll need to pass two hall-pass application requirements. First, do you really need to go from here to there? Getting called out of class to visit the office, advisor, or media center or to deliver something from one teacher to another is approved hall-pass travel. "Needing" to go to the bathroom (again), a locker visit, or faking the need to see the school nurse just as the math test starts are all unapproved travel requests and will be denied. Second, do you respect the power of the pass? Your reputation for past hall-pass behavior can make or break your future pass privileges. The hall pass permits you the privilege to quickly go from point A to point B and back again. Hall passes are not a get-out-of-class pass, releasing you to free-range wander around the school. Respect the pass! Respect it!

## Looking Back

I can now see how teachers could tell if a kid really needed to leave class to use the bathroom or not. They stood in the hall between classes and saw who was playing around and who had stopped at the bathroom. The kids who socialized and didn't visit the bathroom always asked to go during class. So when the teacher said no, they were teaching the kid a lesson about going to the bathroom between classes and not during class.

Cole

MAIN OFFICE

MAIN OFFICE

# HALLWAYS

**H**allways are the highways of school. Routes exist to move the middle school masses and their cargo from one school stop to the next. Like downtown traffic during rush hour, your school hallways will occasionally get all jammed up bumper-to-bumper and even report a few shoe flat-tires and fender-bender backpack accidents. To keep traffic moving, and the hall cops off your tail, follow these basic road rules to arrive at your next destination on time. Always walk on the right side, yield to 8th graders, look both ways when turning toward the lockers—and no speeding! People get furious fast when a couple of punk 6th grade racers think they have license to hall hog and swerve their way through the foot traffic, only to crash into a slower-moving caravan of upperclassmen.

## How To . . .
### Pick Up Your Papers When Dropped in the Hallway

**STEP 1**—Stop, drop, and protect your papers. They are about to get trampled. Don't just stand there and look confused.

**STEP 2**—Scoop up the dropped papers. Don't worry about keeping them in order.

**STEP 3**—Stand back up and keep moving. Hold on to your papers tight so you don't drop them again.

**STEP 4**—Step aside and try to organize the mess of papers you hold. If something is missing, go back and attempt a recovery mission.

# HAND WASHING

**T**hink about all the stuff you touch at school. Your mitts grip doorknobs, handrails, seats, lockers, desks, hall walls, gym floors, and countless other sticky surfaces. Then with filthy fingers you dig around in your bag for a sharp pencil. One minute later you stick that putrid pencil in your mouth. Without thinking about it, you just chewed on a yellow #2 stick of germs, bacteria, and microscopic viruses. One way to combat self-contamination is to wash your hands a couple times a day at school. For sure wash them after every visit to the bathroom, science class, gym class, and trips through the locker room. Think you can handle it?

**True Story**

Dr. Ignaz Semmelweis was the first to wash his hands before operating. He scrubbed in chlorinated limewater to "remove all adhering cadaverous particles." The year was 1846.[11]

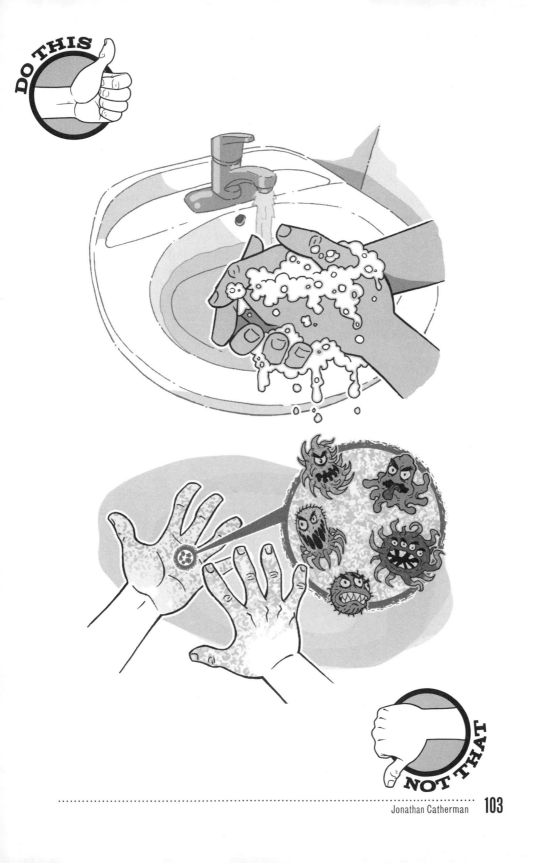

# HANDWRITING

**T**he ancient Egyptians wrote in hard-to-read scripts called *hieroglyphs*. To read and understand their writings requires the keen eye of a trained professional. Well, you're not King Tut and your mummy may need to help with your English homework, so leave the archaeologists in the sand and let's work on your handwriting. For the last six years you have practiced your writing skills, which means you should be pretty good at it by now. Capitalizing letters at the beginning of each sentence, crossing your *t*'s, dotting your *i*'s, and fitting each word between the lines on the paper is exactly what teachers expect of all middle school students. If you still insist on wandering all over the page with your words, scratching out letters that you don't even recognize, and ending sentences with odd-shaped punctuation marks, then move to the desert and chisel your hieroglyphs into the walls of your pyramid. No? Well then, slow your scroll, keep it between the lines, and always remember your penmanship.

## *Just Joking*

**What do you get when you cross a big green monster and a fountain pen?**

The Ink-credible Hulk.

# HOME ROOM

It's been said that a man's home is his castle. You know who lives in castles? Kings. You know who lives in the castle's dark and dirty dungeon? Lazy jokers. Don't be the lazy joker who claims it regal to carpet his room with dirty clothes, molding food, and "lost" homework. Instead, be the master of your kingdom and rule your room with a decree to keep the space clean enough for a royal.

## Strange but True

Two Brooklyn, New York, boys found a 4½-foot python in the cushions of their couch. The problem was, they didn't own a pet snake. After calling the police, who called animal control, the snake was determined to have slithered into the home through a toilet, from parts unknown.[12]

# HOMEROOM

The plan for homeroom is to start the school day off right. Often homeroom time is used for teachers to take attendance, share some announcements, and get ready for the day ahead. Yet some guys feel their homeroom at school is an extension of their room at home. These guys figure if they were home, they would be sleeping, so why not catch some z's at school too? Well, rise and shine, fellas! Think of the school bell that starts homeroom as your second alarm clock, without the snooze option. The sun is up, you are awake, and the school day is ready to go.

**To Do in Middle School:**

✓ Join a club or sport.

# HOMEWORK

**S**ome teachers are all about assigning homework and some are not. Some class subjects require you to read, study, write, or prepare outside of assigned time in school. There is no predicting how often or how much homework middle school will require, but one thing is for certain—it's best to get it done and handed in . . . on time. The crazy but true part is that teachers often see guys "forget" to hand in finished homework more often than they actually forget to finish their homework. That's like going out to dinner, ordering, and paying for the food . . . but forgetting to eat it. Once you get it done, hand it in . . . on time. Oh, and one more thing. Make sure to put your name on your homework before you get it done and handed in . . . on time.

## *Just Joking*

**What did the math book tell the pencil?**

I have a lot of problems.

# LEADERSHIP

**D**o you want to be a leader? Good. You will need to be more influential than you are easily influenced. If you are influential, then you can be a leader. An easy-to-remember definition of leadership is *Leadership is influence, used for good.* Middle school is the prime time to dream, discover, and develop your levels of influence that benefit both yourself and others. First, you'll need to practice self-leadership. Begin with taking responsibility for your own actions and doing what's right, even when nobody is watching. Work hard to get better at what you enjoy, and practice the life skills and moral character that will help you move from where you are to where you need to go. Add in some time management skills and you'll be the leader of you. Second, look for opportunities to lead others. Leading others requires you to treat them as you would want to be treated, listen well, and value teamwork. When others see these values in you, they will want to follow and learn from you. That's when it happens. By using your influence for good, you'll have become a leader.

## Quote

"When you don't criticize others, you're less likely to be criticized. Most people will treat you as you treat them."

Reed

# LOCKDOWNS

As you know, every school must perform lockdown drills. "Lockdown. Lockdown. Lockdown." It may only be a drill, but this is serious stuff. Yet some guys think being the class clown is cool, and the perfect time to make people laugh is when everybody is trying to hide from a bad guy. It's not. Don't be the guy who disrupts the drill by making fake fart sounds, texting a friend, or telling the teacher that you have to go to the bathroom right NOW! Instead, do the right thing and keep calm, follow instructions, stay hidden, remain still, be quiet, and don't mess around. The school receives a grade on how well the drill goes, and the higher the grade the better.

## Ask a Middle School Survivor

**Q:** Are lockdowns the same in middle school as they were in elementary?

**A:** Lockdowns in middle school are pretty much the same as elementary school. It depends on the teacher and school policy. Some teachers may have you get down under a desk. Others may have you hide somewhere else in the classroom. Just do what they say and you'll do fine.

Cole

# LOCKER LOCKS

**M**any guys find it easy to slam their locker door closed, yet a bit more difficult to open it again. The sickening feeling of realizing you've forgotten your locker combination is like the dry heaves prior to puking. A full list of symptoms includes sweaty palms, shortness of breath, blurred vision, shaky hands, dry mouth, stomach pain, and the false feeling of world-ending panic. In an effort to avoid such exaggerated symptoms, follow this two-step procedure:

> **STEP 1**—Memorize your locker combination and practice cracking the code as many times as you need to never forget it. Seriously, drill those numbers so deep into your brain you'll still remember them the day you graduate from high school.

> **STEP 2**—Repeat step 1 until you get it right, every time.

This simple remedy is recommended by 11 out of 9 doctors and should keep you from locking yourself out.

## How To . . .
### Open a Standard Combination Lock

> **Turn #1**—Spin right (clockwise) three full turns. Stop at your FIRST number.

> **Turn #2**—Spin left (counterclockwise) one full turn, passing the FIRST number, and stop at the SECOND number.

> **Turn #3**—Spin right (clockwise) and stop at the THIRD number.

> **Pull open lock.**

# LOCKER ROOMS

**L**ocker rooms are like no other place on earth. Their mighty mix of smells, sounds, and sights can make you question all of humanity. The air grows foul with BO, floors are damp with sweat, and toilets stew with unflushed toxic waste. Basically, short visits are required, but this is no place to hang out. Still, you'll see guys wanting to play, prank, and park themselves on the floor. This is not advisable, considering fungus and fecal matter is festering underfoot in most locker rooms. Your best plan is to get in, get changed, and get out. Be sure to always wash your hands after each visit and change your gym clothes after every use. Finally, a message from the masses: a cologne spray down does not cover your BO. It only makes the smell worse. The only way to cut your stank is with soap and water. Most schools won't make you shower in the locker room, but this doesn't mean you are good to go. Consider hygiene your homework and shower each and every day at home. You may not be able to avoid going to the locker room, but you can avoid smelling like one.

## Ask a Middle School Survivor

**Q:** Why do we need to change clothes in a locker room?

**A:** Because you need to change into your gym clothes somewhere, and changing in a bathroom stall is not an option. Stashing your school clothes and stuff in a locker is a good way to keep your things safe. Just get in, get changed, and get out again. Nobody is watching and nobody cares. Just be sure to wear clean underwear.

Reed

# LOCKERS

**S**ome guys treat a school locker like their future first cheap apartment. Basically a cramped, dark, smelly place just big enough to stash a few things. It's good for short visits but you wouldn't want to stay long. If left unchecked, a locker can get packed so tight with smelly gym clothes, rotting food, and "lost" homework that the health department could have it condemned. Don't be that guy. Be the guy with the cool crib by keeping your locker clean. You may even want to DIY the place by adding a shoe shelf or a few cool pictures.

## Ask a Middle School Survivor

**Q:** How many times a day will I get to go to my locker?

**A:** That depends. Some days you will have a class schedule that requires you to stop by your locker between every class. Other days you might not have enough time to make it to your locker and then go to class. So plan ahead and carry a backpack or multiple subject binder between classes and locker stops. But make sure not to carry too much in your backpack. Over time, a heavy pack will hurt your back.

Reed

# LOST AND FOUND

The middle school lost and found is a strange mix of forgotten valuables and trashed articles. From expensive electronics to pocket trinkets, you would be surprised what gets left behind in class, gym, and on the bus. Here's a short list of real items lost and found in middle school.

## Found

cowboy hat, straw

jacket, size M

mini Statue of Liberty

math binder, algebra

snow pants, blue

fishing pole, no line

black glove, left hand

headphones, red

water bottle, empty

diary, unlocked

belt, brown

eyeglasses, prescription

birthday card, Sarah's 12th

hammock, canvas

beach ball, multicolor

retainer case, with retainer

drumstick, wooden

dog collar, no dog

plastic globe, coin inside

flashlight, no batteries

tree ornament, Christmas

shoe, right

"Found—shoe, right" . . . Really?! Who loses one of two shoes and doesn't notice? How did that guy walk home from school, thinking, "Something feels different. I don't know exactly what, just different." Really, man? Look down. You're missing a shoe! If you find yourself claiming the title of The One-Shoed Wonder or just can't find your jacket, lunch bag, glove, or mini Statue of Liberty, take the time to stop by the school's lost and found. You may have to dig through the collection of unclaimed treasures for your missing jewel. Just remember, finders keepers only applies if it really is yours. There's no "shopping" for five-finger discounts in the lost and found.

## *Just Joking*

Whoever lost a roll of $20 bills wrapped in a rubber band, I found the rubber band.

LOST SHOE

Blue eyes with white laces.
Kind sole but likes to stick tongue out.
Tends to walk off when left unattended.
Last seen standing beside twin in gym class.

PLEASE CALL 555-7463
PLEASE CALL 555-7463
PLEASE CALL 5...
PLEASE CALL 555-7463
PLEA...
PLEASE CALL 555-7463
PLEASE CALL 555-7463

# LUNCH

**E**veryone's heard an adult say, "Don't talk with your mouth full. It's rude." If you can't remember ever hearing such table instructions, you were polite from birth or you forgot—again. Lunchtime is a balance between talking with your friends and eating your food. Your body needs the fuel while your friends need to talk about the latest game hack and online prank video. The good news is you can do both, just not at the same time. The rule is simple: Say it, don't spray it. Eat a few bites. Chew and swallow. Talk for a minute. Take a drink. Swallow. Take another bite. While chewing with your mouth closed, be a good listener to what your friends are saying. Swallow. Talk again. Repeat these simple steps: eat, talk, eat, talk, eat, talk, and you'll finish both your lunch and talking with friends before the bell sends you all back to class.

## True OR False

### Chewing with your mouth open is considered polite in some cultures.

**True.** In some cultures, slurping while drinking and chewing with your mouth open shows the cook or host that you find the food delicious, while in other cultures such behavior would be considered extremely offensive. So be sure to study up before you chow down.

# LUNCH LINE

**N**ext in line. Next in line, please. What do you want for lunch today, sweetie? Fruit with that? A cookie too? How about some milk or juice with your meal? Next in line, please. Next in line."

Making your way through the school lunch line is a lot like selecting a meal at your local fast-food restaurant. True, there are fewer choices, no soda, and you can't megasize a school lunch—but you're still supposed to move fast through the food line. Just like ordering at McJacks or Taco King, it's best to know your options before it's your turn. Waiting to decide until after the lunch lady is staring at you is too late. Make your choice, fill your tray, and don't forget a drink. Finally, don't rush, and no pushing as you head into the lunchroom to find your friends.

## How To . . .
### Pack Your Own Lunch

**STEP 1**—Select leftovers from the refrigerator or make a fresh sandwich.

**STEP 2**—Pick a healthy balance of food that includes a main item, fruit or vegetable, and a treat. Don't forget a bottle of water.

**STEP 3**—Put each food item into a sealed plastic bag or approved food container.

**STEP 4**—Pack all your lunch items in a lunch bag or box. Add an ice pack if you've got perishables, like meat or dairy or mayo.

# LYING

**G**ood thing the childish taunt "Liar, liar, pants on fire" is far from factual. If it were a statement of the obvious, how often would smoke trail up from behind you following a fib? One thing is for certain: When you lie, you're going to get burned. Teachers, principals, coaches, and even bus drivers are really good at turning up the heat when they know your story lacks honesty. Chances are they have heard the same tall tale told before and recognize your false testimony for what it really is. A lie. So face the facts and be truthful. Honestly, it's much cooler.

## *Just Joking*

**Never trust an atom. They make up everything.**

# MEDIA CENTER/ LIBRARY

**S**ee those rectangular things on the shelf? Those are called books. They are like TV for smart people. The media center has them stacked all over the place. Those machines on the tables are computers. Like books, they too can open doors to discovery, lead to great adventures, and be your ticket to more information than any one person could consume in their lifetime. Or, the media center may seem like slow, quiet torture for the middle school student who thinks they already know all they need to succeed. Why read when there's a video? Why study when Google knows all the answers? Why, why, why? Well, because only a fool hates wisdom and learning. And you're no fool. So enjoy a little quiet time and crack the cover of a book, and use a computer for more than gaming. You never know what you'll discover.

## To Do in Middle School:

✓ Find and visit with a couple of your favorite teachers from grades past. Thank them for all they taught you and share your current successes with them.

# MONEY

**M**oney is like magic. With a simple distraction and sleight of hand, it can disappear into thin air. Now you see it. *Poof!* Now you don't. And what do you have left? An empty soda, some candy wrappers, and a bad case of what feels like indigestion but is really buyer's remorse from getting what you didn't need and now don't want. The trick to managing money in middle school is figuring out how cash works more like a tool and less like candy. "Yeah, but I like candy," is what you're thinking—and you're right, who doesn't?

The truth is, the older you get, the bigger and more expensive the things you buy get. So now is the time to master your money and stop believing the illusion that your money grows as you do. The fact is, you are running out of teeth to put under your pillow, the few bucks your grandparents slip into a birthday card only comes around once a year, and your parents are not an open bank vault. What money you can make from mowing lawns, dog sitting, or doing your share of work around the house can be put to work for you. Here's how: Save in the bank as much as you can, spend as little as you must, and give to charity as if you were the one in need. This makes you the master of your money and keeps you from being mastered by money's many sweet illusions.

 **Quote**

"The art is not in making money, but in keeping it."

—Proverb

# NAIL TRIMMING

According to the Guinness World Records, the man with the longest fingernails ever was a guy from Pontiac, Michigan, named Melvin Boothe.[13] The combined length of his 10 fingernails was over 32 feet long. That's an average of 16 feet per hand or 38 inches per finger. Not so great for playing catch, but you can bet he could scratch every inch of his back. Don't be the long-nailed version of Melvin at your school. Keep your fingernails trimmed and whatever you do, NO biting! Want some handsome hands? Read "How to Trim Your Fingernails" in *The Manual to Manhood*.

## Strange but True

Lots of germs and some nasty bacteria live under your fingernails. What kind, you ask? The kind that hang on after making a trip to the bathroom, tugging off gym socks, or petting your dog. Think about that fun fact next time you nibble on your nails.

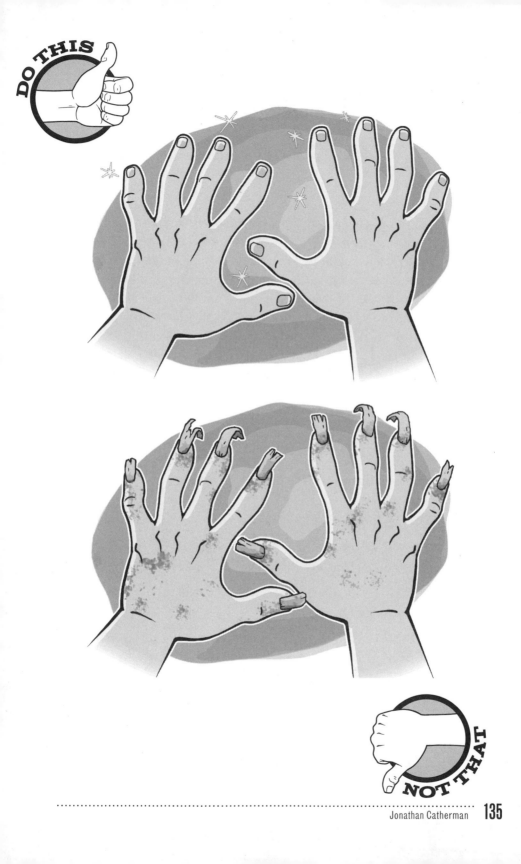

# NAME ON YOUR PAPER

**Y**ou did all that homework. You studied, researched, and worked hard to write a great paper. You stuffed it into your backpack, went to school, and even remembered to turn it in on time. A few days later the teacher hands back the graded assignments and yours is "missing." She points you to a stack of papers on her desk and there you discover your work. Graded down from a B+ to C+. What the what!? Then you see it. Across the top of the page is written, "No name." Oh man! You forgot to put your name on the top of the page! Seriously? After all that hard work, you forgot the simplest part of the assignment? The only part you are guaranteed to get right? Come on, man! Name it and claim it. Always remember to put your name on the paper before handing it in.

## How To . . .
### Remember Somebody's Name

**STEP 1**—Introduce yourself. Tell them your name and ask theirs.

**STEP 2**—Repeat their name in your head and in a sentence. Like this: "You said your name is Shawn? Nice to meet you, Shawn."

**STEP 3**—Try to associate them with somebody else you know with the same name.

**STEP 4**—Use their name whenever you talk with them. This will burn their name into your memory.

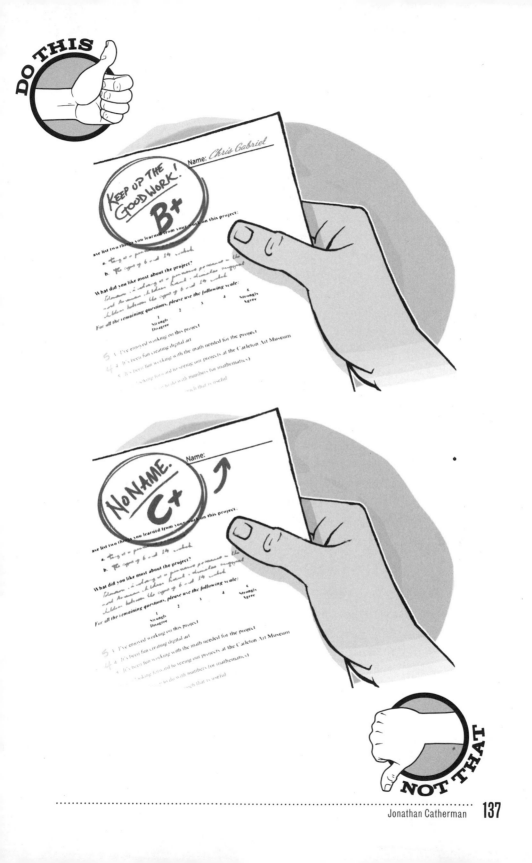

# ONLINE

Do you know what WWW stands for? If you guessed Wide World of Wrestling, you're right! Not really. Sorry. Actually, you'd be way off. The truth is, back in 1983, researchers began assembling a computer-based "network of networks" to share data between universities and government organizations around the globe. This early version of what would become the internet wasn't very cool until 1990 when a British computer scientist named Tim Berners-Lee, also known as TimBL, invented the World Wide Web. From then to now, the interweb has spun from telephone landline dial-up to wireless go-anywhere connectivity. People used to "go online" occasionally. Today you live much of your life online. From googling "who is TimBL" to the GPS location tracker on your phone, you are leaving digital footprints, fingerprints, and imprints everywhere you virtually and actually go. This can make your life easier or bring it crashing back to reality. Keep your surfing pure and you'll be cool with your teachers, parents, future college applications, and job interviews. Remember, it's important that you never share personal information about yourself online! Go rogue while wired and you'll have some explaining to do about what your little eyes have seen, thumbs have clicked, and where you were online when that spyware accidently infected your device.

## Strange but True
The first website went live way back in 1991. It is dedicated to information about the World Wide Web and is still active today. You can check it out for yourself at http://info.cern.ch/hypertext/WWW/TheProject.html.

# PARENTS

Chances are when your parents were in middle school, there were no seat belt laws, bike helmets, bottled water, smartphones, social media, reality TV, or online prank videos. Their idea of password protection was a secret phrase whispered in a friend's ear before entering a tree fort or cushion castle. A lot has changed since your parents were in middle school, so you'll have to give them a break every now and then when they just don't understand. Really, parenting is no easy task. Few other adventures in life can bring more joy or pain to a person than the responsibility and privilege of parenting. You'll want to add to the privilege they have of raising you by scoring some positive points with the parental units as often as possible. Here are two of the best ways: Spend time with them and talk to them. Time spent together and talking about stuff, or through stuff, is how good relationships are built. The better your relationship, the happier both you and your parents will be. They may not know what it's like to be in middle school today, but you can teach them. They may or may not agree with all you share, but you'll be amazed how smart they become by the time you're a parent and your kids are in middle school.

## Quote

"A child who is allowed to be disrespectful to his parents will not have true respect for anyone."[14]

—Billy Graham

# PDA

4COL, PDA is so JV and needs to stop PDQ! HAK in public qualifies as TMI! That just DNC. Just because you have a BCO your G/F, it doesn't mean we want to CU SWALK your T<3 between math and geography class. TBH and UFN middle school is a bit early to DTR by telling somebody 143 and exchanging 88 A3. Instead, SC and try JBF instead of standing FTF in the middle of the hall. Besides, the HL of most middle school couples is one WK, maybe two. You can GA and like the GRL. Just don't show PDA.

## Ask a Middle School Survivor

How do I understand all the abbreviations girls keep messaging me?

143 = I love you

4COL = for crying out loud

88 = hugs and kisses

A3 = anytime, anywhere, anyplace

AYS = are you serious

BCO = big crush on

CU = see you

DNC = does not compute

DTR = define the relationship

FTF = face-to-face

GA = go ahead

G/F = girlfriend

GRL = girl

HAK = hugs and kisses

HL = half-life

JBF = just being friends

JV = junior varsity

PDA = public displays of affection

PDQ = pretty darn quick

SC = stay cool

SWALK = sealed with a loving kiss

T<3 = true love

TBH = to be honest

TMI = too much information

UFN = until further notice

URW = you are welcome

WK = week

XOXOXO = hugs and kisses

*Reed*

# PHYSICAL EDUCATION

**S**ome guys look forward to PE class as a welcome break from the rear-numbing job of desk jockey. Other guys walk to gym class thinking, "I'm really more of the brainiac type." Well, guess what? Jock or not, exercise boosts the brain's power. Guys who move more than their mouth outperform sofa surfers in simple tasks like "long-term memory, reasoning, attention, and problem solving."[15] It's true, look it up. That, and a healthy young man like yourself is capable of walking about 12 miles a day without feeling the pain. Unless you haven't moved that far in weeks, which means you're probably growing tired from just holding this book. Look at it this way. Physical education class is way more than running, jumping, and doing sports-like stuff a few times a week. Exercising your body builds your muscle strength, physical coordination, and brain-processing power. Put all those benefits together, and it's good to know that if the zombie apocalypse ever does come, you'll be able to both outthink and outrun the walking dead.

Cole

### Looking Back

Wearing the dirty gym clothes I pulled out of the bottom of my bag was never a good sight or smell. I learned the hard way that re-wearing week-old gym clothes could almost kill me by asphyxiation. That kind of smell should be illegal. I know now to wash my gym clothes after every use.

# POP QUIZZES

Okay, everybody. Please put your books away, sharpen a pencil, and prepare to take an unscheduled test.

**Question #1—What is the secret to passing pop quizzes in middle school?**

"No, no, don't tell me. I know this one."

The answer is _____*(Fill in the blank)*

Or would you prefer to try your luck with multiple-choice answers?

(A) I studied for this all week.

(B) I looked at the chapter practice questions last night for 3 minutes.

(C) I cheat off the answers of the kid sitting next to me.

(D) All of the above.

**Answer: (A)** There is no need to question the fact that middle school is a virtual minefield of both expected and surprisingly too-frequent "I didn't know we had a quiz today!" tests. From the weekly exam to pop quizzes that come out of nowhere, the only answer to passing tests in class and life is to study ahead and be prepared for the unexpected. Good luck.

Correction . . . good studying.

## Looking Back

Asking the teacher, "Is this going to be on the test?" was never a very good question. They always said something like, "You will just have to take the test to find out." Once I started studying like everything the teacher taught might be on the test is when I started getting good grades on the tests.

Cole

# PREPARED FOR CLASS

**Y**ou beat the bell and made it to class on time. Now, are you prepared for class to start? Ask any teacher and they will agree the top 10 things you need to bring to class each day include

1. Pencil (with eraser)
2. Pen (blue or black)
3. Lined paper (wide or college ruled, depending on the class)
4. Completed homework (finished before class starts)
5. Class textbook (when provided)
6. School-provided technology (charged and ready to go)
7. Calculator (a must for math and science)
8. Personal technology (if allowed)
9. Rested eyes (that means sleeping in your bed, at night, and not in class)
10. Self-motivation, confidence, drive, grit, humility, manners, and a willingness to learn (okay, that's seven unique traits, but just saying "character" wouldn't do)

## True OR False

**It's the teacher's job to hand out pencils to whoever forgot one.**

**False.**

# PRINCIPAL

**W**ho's the boss? You know, the big shot, big cheese, bigwig, big kahuna? Kingpin, kingfish, King Kong? Top dog, top brass, guru, all pro, CEO? Who's the brains around here? The principal is, of course. But why? What have they done to deserve the leader of leaders title? Well, most public school principals have earned at least a master's if not a doctoral degree. That means they were in school as a student for somewhere between 17 and 19 years before getting the job. That doesn't even count the years of experience they had in the classroom as a teacher or in the front office as a vice principal. It's a pretty good bet that they've been around school longer than you've been alive. It's also pretty safe to say they chose to work in middle school because they like you. "But, what's not to like?" you ask. Really? Middle school administration is not the easiest way to make a living. Your principal has to deal with a limitless flow of drama, crazy hormones, know-it-alls, and a daily dose of "What just happened here?" To make both your day and theirs the best it can be, try introducing yourself to the principal. Let them know you appreciate them and all they do for the school. Sound strange? Come on, this is middle school. You can do it. And don't worry. The principal may be the top dog around campus, but they don't bite.

## True OR False

**Some principals are so committed to their job they sleep at the school.**

**True.** A principal in Asotin, Washington, told his students that if they could raise $10,000 in the school fundraiser, he would sleep on the school roof overnight. Students raised $22,000 in pledges, and Mr. Nicholas slept on the roof, in a tent, in a sleeping bag, in the middle of October.[16]

# PROBLEM SOLVING

One of the biggest differences between immature and mature middle school students is their ability to problem solve. Immature students need their teachers, parents, and friends to solve all their problems. Mature students work to resolve their problems on their own the best way they know how. Immature people say stuff like, "I can't do the work because I don't have a pencil." Mature problem solvers ask a friend for a pencil before the test begins. When two students fight over who gets to sit by the window during a science lab, they are immature. When they work together to move two chairs together on the window side of the lab table, they are mature. If "You didn't tell me what homework I missed when I was absent" has ever crossed your lips and assaulted a teacher's ears . . . yep, you guessed it. Immature. By telling the teacher, "I missed class yesterday and am looking for what homework was assigned," you demonstrate your maturity level and ability to problem solve.

**True Story**

"Houston, we have a problem." In 1970 the manned space mission of Apollo 13 had a massive malfunction in their $CO_2$ filter system. The lives of three astronauts hung in the balance unless a solution could be found. Working together, a team of problem solvers back on earth found a way to fit a square filter into a round hole. Their "get 'er done" efforts saved the Apollo crew and made for a great story, which was scripted into the blockbuster movie *Apollo 13*.

# PUBERTY

As much as your school life is changing, so is your body. Thanks to puberty, your voice will soon begin to crack in mid-sentence as you drop a few octaves. A daily shower becomes a must for those who wish to avoid exposing the world to the toxic smell of their sour pits. Hair will sprout out of your legs and arms and in places you guard like PRIVATE PROPERTY. Your shoulders will widen, your feet will grow, and zits will become your sworn enemy. Seriously, all this and more is headed your way if it hasn't already started. The good news about puberty is that it's an important part of you becoming a man. Nobody wants to stay a boy forever, except Peter Pan and he's not real. Middle school is no fairy tale and puberty isn't the horror movie some make it out to be. What can you do to make the most of this awkward yet important stage of life? Don't fight it. Embrace the changes and take care of yourself, man. He who welcomes his "making of a man" transformation will find the end result to be well worth the effort.

## Pop Quiz

**Q:** How old are most boys when they begin puberty?

**A:** The first signs of puberty in boys usually start at about 11 or 12 years old.

# RAISE YOUR HAND

**O**oh, ooh, ooh, call on me. Call on me. I know it. I know this one. I know. Over here. Right here. Me, me, me. Call on MEEEE!!!!!!"

There you are, waving your arms around, hands raised high, and you know the teacher can hear you begging for a chance to be heard. But nooooo. They call on the kid sitting over there all calm, hand barely raised over their head. That or the teacher calls on the kid who's not even raising his hand. What the what? Well, let's see if you know the answer to this one, smart guy. Are you pushy? Do you ever blurt out the answer? Do you have an expert opinion for every question the teacher asks? Or let's consider the opposite. Do you hide in the back of class and avoid all contact with the teacher? When you are asked a question, do you shrug it off and mumble, "I dunno . . ."?

Let's go with this. It's a good idea to raise your hand from time to time, when you know the answer. But it's never good to be a know-it-all, all the time. Guys who try to sit all quiet hoping not to be noticed will eventually be asked to speak up. Chances are the one time the teacher does volunteer you to share is the exact time you don't know what the teacher is talking about. Your best plan is to raise your hand with an answer when you know the answer, at least once a day. It's not hard. Simply lift your hand over your head and make eye contact with the teacher. When they call on you, share what you know. It's also good to raise your hand to ask good questions every now and then. If you don't get what the teacher is teaching, put that hand up and ask a question. Ask good questions and you will get good answers. Ask shallow questions and you can expect shallow answers. Ask no questions and you will get no answers.

## How To . . .
### Fake an Answer

**STEP 1**—Trick question! Your teacher already knows the answer to the question they just asked. Do you really think they are new to this? Seriously, they are a credentialed pro and you're just trying to fake it. Nice try, Joe.

# READING FOR FUN

**G**uys who read can go anywhere, do anything, and be anyone they choose. Readers transport through time from ancient days to futuristic fantasies. Readers have seen the glory of a hero's adventure and the intrigue of true mystery. Readers have looked out over a sea of adoring fans chanting their name and stood alone against the wrath of an enemy determined to destroy. Readers fly on the back of dragons and explore the depths of space. Readers are the first to discover and the last to abandon their imagination. Guys who read can travel the world, save the universe, and live a thousand lives before finishing middle school. Guys who never read will live only once.

## Quote

"Not all readers are leaders, but all leaders are readers."[17]

—Harry Truman, the 33rd president
of the United States (1945–1953)

# READING FOR SCHOOL

Okay, here's the situation. Your homework this weekend is to read chapters 8 and 9 in your earth science book. On Monday morning there will be a closed book test worth 10% of your final grade. What will you do? If you're thinking it's a good plan to read the chapters and take notes about the important parts, then you are setting yourself up for success come test time. If you are thinking the reading is dumb and taking notes is a waste of time because there are no important parts, um . . . good luck with that. A good plan is to finish the assigned reading before the assigned time. How you do this is up to you, but do plan your reading and work your plan. Some guys like to just "get 'er done" all at once. Others prefer to read for a few minutes here, a few minutes there, and then push through with an hour of no interruptions and good note taking. Try a few strategies till you find the one that helps the reading stick with you. Remember, just pushing through the words does you no good if you can't recall what they said. You never know, you might just read something new and cool enough to remember after the test.

## Ask a Middle School Survivor

**Q:** If the middle school assigns summer reading, what happens when I don't read the book?

**A:** You will get a bad grade on the very first day. That's not a good way to start the year. I recommend you do a little bit of the reading each week over the summer.

Cole

# REPORT CARDS

**R**eport cards are a lot like sports scores. How a team performs on the field or court shows up on the scoreboard without bias. That means no coach, official, or fan can just toss up or take off points to make a team look better or worse than they actually performed. The same is true about your report card. Teachers can't just "give" you a good or bad grade. What they post in report cards is an accounting of how you performed in their class. Basically, you did the work and they kept the score. If you want to keep score too, you can. In fact a good game plan includes you knowing how well you are doing in a class day to day. Most middle schools give you access to an online grade book where you and your parents can see what assignments are handed in, which are missing, the grades you've earned, test scores, and extra credit points. You'll be able to see, track, and predict what your score will be come report card day. This way you can own your own grades and not just wait for the end of the game to learn the score.

## To Do in Middle School:

✓ Make AB Honor Roll.

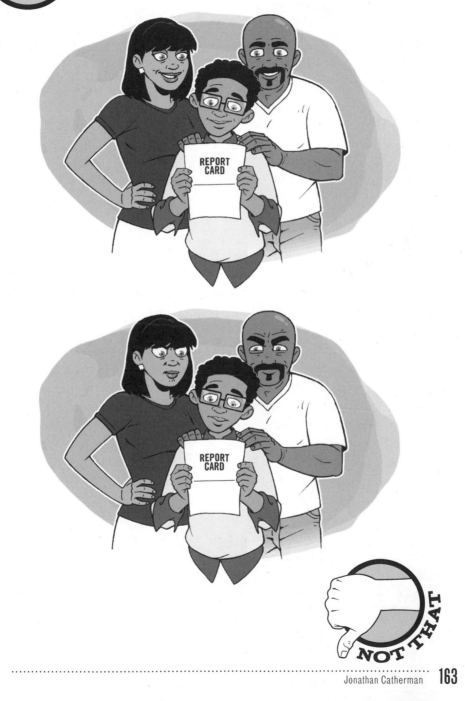

# RESPECT UPPERCLASSMEN

**F**ear and respect are two different things. You have no need to fear the students in the grades above you. Yet, showing them respect is a must. The best advice is simply to treat your "elders" like you would want to be treated. Show them some respect by being polite and staying cool when they are around, and they are more likely to be good to you too.

### True Story

When I was in middle school, I admired the guy who lived down the street from my house. His name was Chris and he was a few years older than me. When he moved up to high school, everybody thought he was really cool and he became popular fast. One weekend he invited me to go with him to a Friday night high school game. There I was in Chris's car, sitting between two high school girls, and everybody treated me like I was just another one of Chris's cool friends. He made me feel so important and like it was normal for me to hang out with him. This helped me feel comfortable around his friends and encouraged me to act more mature. Many years later I was on a trip visiting the same town where Chris lived with his wife and kids. I stopped in for a visit and to thank him for treating me so nice years before. He said, "Why not. You were totally respectful of my friends and me. I knew I had nothing to worry about. Glad you had a good time. I only wish we had won the game that night."

Jonathan

# SCHOOL PICTURES

**L**ook at the camera and smile. This is for the yearbook, not a mug shot. Posing for a school picture is nothing new to you. You've been doing it since you were in kindergarten. The difference now is that the picture captured in middle school will not just get mailed out to grandparents to be framed or hung on their fridge—that pic is also going into the yearbook. Come the end of the school year, that book will hold you forever captive between the two kids with last names alphabetically beside yours. So what are you going to do on picture day? Might you consider wearing clothes that are both cool and clean? Perhaps brush your teeth and do your hair that day? Maybe even shower and shave if need be? It's up to you. Not like people are going to keep that school picture forever. Oh wait, yes they will. Smile.

## Looking Back

No matter what you do, that picture will look dated one day. I put lots of energy into looking cool on picture day, and then a year later I wondered, "What was I thinking?" Good thing I was okay with changing a lot as I moved through middle school.

Reed

# SHAVING

**B**efore you head into the halls of middle school, I mustache you a question. Have you taken a good look at your face in a mirror lately? See anything besides Cheeto dust on your upper lip? If not, you soon will. Now is about the time the peach fuzz just below your nose starts to turn darker, grow longer, and begin to look like lip moss. Patches of odd-length beardness will soon grow on your cheeks and catlike whiskers may randomly sprout out of your chin. When this happens, don't freak out. You're not turning into a yeti just yet. Instead you have been infected with puberty and it's time to consider your first shave. Until then, don't worry if your mug is free from facial follicles. It won't be long before scraping precision-cut, overpriced steel blades across your tender skin will become a daily test of your blood-letting avoidance skills.

 **Quote**

"I like shaving with a dull razor."

—No man ever

**168**    The Manual to Middle School

# SHOWERING

You know what really stinks about middle school? Middle schoolers. *BOOM!* Truth bomb explodes. More like stink bomb detonated. And who knows, if you're body is found to oppose the nose, somebody may ID your BO as public enemy #1. But wait. I smell more to the story, and it's not all roses. Think logically. By the time a parent, teacher, friend, random weirdo, or pack of vicious girls suggests your soiled self needs a cleaning, how many other people were exposed to your toxic atmosphere? Only one person was brave, or socially insensitive, enough to say something. What can you do to avoid the embarrassment of being the stinky kid? Here's a good plan. It's time to start showering. Every day! In fact, showering daily is part of moving up in life. An unwashed middle school body can quickly become encased in a dingy layer of dirt of the day, sweat, and tweenage hormones. Soap, shampoo, water, and a clean towel are the only true way to refresh your natural self and keep people from pinching their noses when you walk their way.

## Pop Quiz

**Q:** Why does washing with soap work better than just washing with water?
- (A) Magic.
- (B) Soap allows insoluble particles to become soluble in water, so they can then be rinsed away.
- (C) Because my mom says so.
- (D) Both A & C.

**A:** (B) Soap allows insoluble particles to become soluble in water, so they can then be rinsed away.[18]

# SIBLINGS

**O**lder, younger, twins, half, or step, the classification of relation and age range between you and your sibling(s) matters little. The fact is, by the time you are in middle school, you'll have spent about 33% of your spare time with your siblings. That means you have hung out with your stinking brother or crazy sister more than with your friends, teachers, parents, or even by yourself.[19] The quality of the time you spend together probably ranges from hugs to thugs. One minute you are best friends, the next mortal enemies, and then back to good by dinner. You share looks and a last name, a branch on the family tree, and maybe even a room in the house. The most important thing about dealing with your siblings is learning that as you grow older, they aren't going to be important people in your life—they'll be some of the *most important* people in your life.

## True OR False

### Some twins can be the same and the opposite at the same time.

**True.** Some twins are mirror twins. This means they have the same physical features but on opposite sides of their bodies. If one twin is right-handed, the other is left. Some mirror twins can even have mirror organs. One's heart is on the left and their twin's heart is on the right. Even their skeletal features can be reversed.[20]

# SICK DAYS

**S**ick or not sick? That is the question. If you are, stay home. Nobody at school needs to be exposed to your clammy hands and pre-puke face. If you're not really feeling raunchy, don't lick your palms or groan with fake symptoms in an attempt to dodge some test you "don't feel good" about taking. Believe it or not, you have a limited number of sick days before passing a class or grade level becomes a real headache. When you do miss school for a day or two after yacking into the porcelain throne, bring a parent's or doctor's note to the office with an explanation of your absence. And to all you actors out there, keep this fun fact in mind: Once you've faked being sick a few times, nothing short of barfing up a lung will convince people you really do need bed rest.

## True Story

### THE KISSING DISEASE

The 8th grade was the best two years of my middle school life. Seriously, I repeated the 8th grade because I'd been absent for two months, sick with mononucleosis. This energy-draining illness is also known by the shortened title "mono" and its nickname, favored by my friends, the "kissing" disease. I liked my buddy's nonclinical diagnosis the best because it cast me as the one and only guy in our group of friends who had actually kissed a girl. (She would have been a sick girl, but a girl with willing lips nonetheless.) The problem was, I had no idea how I acquired the illness. My lips had no puckering experience, and in fact I would not kiss a girl for another year, at least.

Jonathan

# SKIPPING SCHOOL

**W**hat's the big deal? It's not like skipping school is illegal or anything. Well, actually . . . it is. Skipping school is legally called *truancy* and truancy is illegal for middle school students. Decide not to come to school and you'll rack up an unexcused absence. Unexcused absences add up to makeups, including detention, Saturday school, summer school, and even fines issued to your parents. "Yeah, but school takes up so much time and I never really learn anything anyway," you say. Okay, smart guy, let's do the math and see what you know.

There are 365 days in a year, totaling 8,760 hours. The average student goes to school for about 6½ hours a day, 180 days a year. That totals out to about 1,170 hours per year in school. On average you'll sleep 7 hours a day,[21] totaling 2,555 hours a year. Nine hours a day will be connected to media,[22] ticking up to around 3,285 digital hours per year. You'll spend about 30 minutes a day in the bathroom, flushing away 182 hours a year taking care of business. Now, if you've been keeping track, that leaves you with about 1,568 hours per year to do whatever you do in addition to going to school. That and let's be honest here. All those media minutes you probably spent multitasking while doing other things, so you really have more "free time" than expected. It's basic math. Skipping school is illegal and doesn't add up to be a very valuable way to spend your time. Then again, smart guys like you who go to school know this because you've learned how to do the math.

## *Just Joking*

A mother realizes her son has not gotten out of bed for school. She goes into his room and tells him to get up or he will miss breakfast.

"No," the son replies. "I don't wanna go to school!"

"You HAVE to go to school," the mother scolds.

"No!" he says. "The kids are mean to me, the teachers don't like me, and the lunches are disgusting."

"You WILL go to school, young man," the mother warns.

"Why? Why do I have to go to school today?" the son asks.

"Because you're the principal, now get out of bed!" she says.

# SOCIAL MEDIA

**M**uch *Ado About Nothing* is a play penned by William Shakespeare back in the way late 1500s. It's still popular today with middle school English teachers, so you may be reading it soon. The word *ado* means trouble or difficulty, and that's what the play is all about. Much of the ado in the play comes from a few handwritten letters that cause confusion, gossip, and misdeeds to spread quickly. If Shakespeare were writing the play today, he might exchange those handwritten letters with modern-day social media posts. Seems realistic, considering most people's social media posts are much *to-do* about nothing and easily cause much *ado* about nothing. Think of the time we spend paying attention to what took somebody next to no time to post. Here's a simple Shakespeare-approved line worth memorizing. It may just keep you out of much ado in future social media posts: "Not everyone needs to know everything about you."

## True OR False

### Internet Addiction Disorder (IAD) affects up to 8.2% of the population in the US and Europe.

**True.** Many teenagers use social media and believe it's an important part of their lives. Yet some can get addicted to social media, causing their virtual life to negatively affect their real-world relationships and responsibilities. As powerful as alcohol and drug addiction is, IAD includes social media addiction as a real thing, which may require professional intervention.[23]

# SPORTS

In middle school you'll have your first opportunity to play on a school sports team. Some of the guys who show up for tryouts will have played in rec leagues for years, while others are giving the game their first shot. There is no guarantee the guy with more experience will make the team. Coaches are looking for team members who want to play, are teachable, and are willing to work hard to get better. Sure, raw talent is good, but ask any seasoned pro and they'll tell you exactly what it takes to win: "Hard work beats talent when talent doesn't work hard." So get out there and run, jump, shoot, hit, throw, pin, spike, and sweat your guts out. Make the team, and you can expect to win some games and lose some. What matters most in sports is not the ranking of your team, size of the trophies, or who scores the most points. What matters most is how you play the game as a TEAM. Together Everyone Achieves More.

## Pop Quiz

**Q:** When were the first Olympic Games held?

(A) 1910

(B) 1896

(C) 776 BC

**A:** (C) 776 BC. "The first ancient Olympic Games can be traced back to 776 BC. They were dedicated to the Olympian gods and were staged on the ancient plains of Olympia. They continued for nearly 12 centuries, until Emperor Theodosius decreed in AD 393 that all such 'pagan cults' be banned." [24]

# STEALING

**Guy #1:** "Finders keepers, losers weepers."

**Guy #2:** "Yeah, but you found those headphones inside my backpack."

**Guy #1:** "Don't try to confuse things with a technicality."

Isn't it interesting how "finders keepers" seems to always work in the favor of the "finder"? Then when something of theirs gets "borrowed," they feel horribly wronged and believe the entire world is out to get them. Seriously, man? There are no five-fingered discounts in middle school or beyond. Seeing something you want and just taking it is stealing. We have a law here on planet Earth that basically says, "Thou shall not steal." Also known as theft, robbery, lifting, forced sharing, or borrowing without permission, stealing is stealing. But why do some students feel so entitled to "claim" other people's stuff? Because they lack personal integrity. When a guy has integrity, your stuff is safe around him because he too believes in doing the right thing, even when no one is watching. Be that guy.

## Quote

"Integrity is doing the right thing, even when no one is watching."

—Unknown

# STUDYING

Today is Monday. The test is on Friday. When will you study? The right answer is *A little bit each night*. The wrong answer is *Tomorrow*. It's easy to find at least fifty excuses for why today is not a good day to study. You're busy, tired, hungry, bored, brain-dead, or rebelling against the system. Besides, you'll just cram the night before and ace that test on Friday. Fail. Here are a few study tips from professional brain scientists who know a thing or two about how the mind of a middle school student works. If you want to ace the test, try these study strategies on for size:

1. **Break it up**—Turn your study sessions into mini-lessons. Don't try to memorize the names of all the state capitals in one sitting. Instead, learn a few every day over a few days. Be sure to review what you learned last before starting the next set.[25]

2. **Move around**—Try studying the same stuff in a different place next time. You are more likely to remember the name of the state capitals when you move from studying in the library to your kitchen table, to the backyard, or to the gym after basketball practice. This forces your brain to form new associations with the same information, and that makes your memory sticky.[26]

3. **Work it out**—Getting some aerobic exercise builds more than your muscles. Research shows that running a couple laps around the house or doing a few jumping jacks between study questions will improve your brain-processing speed.[27]

## True OR False

**By sleeping with a book under your pillow, the information will infiltrate your brain while you dream.**

**False.** Dream on.

# SUBSTITUTE TEACHERS

**S**tudents say lots of things about substitute teachers. Some of what they say is true. Most of it isn't.

"I hear we have Mr. Garvey as a substitute in math today. My friend's brother's locker partner was in band class with a kid who says Mr. Garvey is really nice and that he thinks homework should be illegal, so he never gives it. I'm going to love him."

"I hear we have Mrs. Smith as a substitute in PE today. My sister knows this kid who used to go to school here but moved last year and she said Mrs. Smith was a Marine Drill Sergeant and gives people detention if they can't do 50 push-ups. I hate her already."

"I hear we have Miss Holly as a substitute in history today. I heard this 8th grader say twice that she shows kung fu movies in class and keeps the ashes of her dead dog in the backseat of her car. She is so weird."

Before you believe everything you hear about a substitute teacher, consider giving them the same break you know they would give you. Instead of being quick to judge, try getting to know them a little bit first. You may be surprised to learn most substitute teachers are pretty normal people, doing a really tough job, for not much pay.

## Ask a Middle School Survivor

**Q:** Are substitute teachers out to get you in middle school?

**A:** Some subs may seem like they don't like you, but they really are there to help, not hurt you. If they seem frustrated, it's probably because some kid is annoying them. Was it you? Don't be annoying.

Cole

# SWEARING

There are 191 four-letter words in the English language that start with the letter *f*. Most are *fine*, yet a few are particularly *foul* and should *fail* to ever *flow from* your *face*. In its simplest *form* you'll *find* cursing, swearing, profanity, blasphemy, and vulgarity all *flop flat* and *fall* to the lowest *form* of spoken expression. President Abraham Lincoln once said that it's "better to remain silent and be thought a *fool* than to speak out and remove all doubt."[28] Sure, dropping a *fury* of "f-bombs" in a *free-flow furl* of *foul flak* is *fuel* for *fake fame from fain fans*, but in *fact*, it's never clever. Verbally shocking *folk* with the *fail* of *foul* language is like playing in traffic. It's guaranteed to get people's attention *fast*, but in the end, the *fool* will *feel* the greatest pain.

## Quote

"I had three rules, pretty much, that I stuck with practically all the time. . . . I believe in starting on time, and I believe closing on time. And another one I had was, not one word of profanity. One word of profanity, and you are out of here for the day. If I see it in a game, you're going to come out and sit on the bench. And the third one was, never criticize a teammate."[29]

—Coach John Wooden, American basketball player and coach

As head coach at UCLA he won ten NCAA national championships in a 12-year period, including a record seven in a row.

# TEACHERS

Recent advancements in human research have discovered a remarkable fact about student and teacher interactions. When exposed to powerful doses of the positively charged element Hu+, teachers often absorb the contagious properties of kindness in high concentrations. Hu+ then reproduces rapidly in the exposed subject and is released again by reverse osmosis toward students in close proximity. This amazing finding may sound impossible, yet in test after test the evidence is conclusive. Put simply, when a student is nice to a teacher, the teacher will be nice back to the student. Often referred to as The Golden Rule experiment, you can test the method for yourself, on yourself. Your findings could change the world as you know it.

### True Story

Before he became the mega celebrity for his roles on stage and in movies like *X-Men*, Hugh Jackman was a school gym teacher. One of Mr. Jackman's former students was Rollo Ross, who grew up to become an entertainment reporter. As luck would have it, Rollo Ross got the opportunity to interview his former teacher at a red-carpet event. Just as Rollo started the interview, the teacher in Mr. Jackman came out. "Rollo, I'm sorry, mate," Mr. Jackman interrupted, "but we go way back. I used to teach you at a high school in PE, and I want to know how your physical education is progressing. It's very important to me." Mr. Jackman continued and totally surprised Rollo with a pop quiz when he asked, "How is your education going? Did I set you up for life?" Luckily for Rollo, the Wolverine was in a good mood and enjoyed joking around with his former student.[30]

# TESTING

**T**ests are part of school—and life. Some students say stuff like, "I'm good at math, just not at taking tests." Okay, let's compare this test-taking trouble to life outside the classroom. Can a football team's quarterback be good at throwing the ball, just not during the game? Or what if a musician claimed to be a great rapper, just not when performing. How about a doctor who knows all about healing but forgets what to do during surgery. The trick to how pros perform under pressure is similar to how you can set yourself up for test-taking success. The pros have performance strategies and good students do too. Here's a tried-and-true plan for you.

## Test prep

- Study well in advance of the test.
- Get a good night's sleep before the test.
- Eat a good breakfast and drink some water.

## Test taking

- Listen to the teacher's instructions.
- Read each question or passage all the way through before answering.
- Answer the questions you know first.
- When you don't know an answer, eliminate options you think are wrong.

## Test completion

- Use any time you have left to double-check your work.
- Make sure your name is on the test.

---

### Pop Quiz

**Q:** 111111111
$$x\ \underline{111111111}$$

**A:** 1234567898 7654321

# TEXTING

On December 3, 1992, a 22-year-old test engineer named Neil sat at his computer and sent the first SMS text message to his friend Richard's phone. The message shared between the friends was a holiday greeting that read "Merry Christmas."[31] What started with one message in 1992 is now estimated to be 23 billion messages sent per day. That's over 16 million messages per minute. This means there's no escaping the short messages, and that can be a problem for you in middle school. Here's why. Splitting your attention between two or more tasks is called *multitasking*. Homework and texting is multitasking. Studying and texting is multitasking. Riding a bike and texting is multitasking. Walking and texting is multitasking. The problem is, our brains can't do either well when we try to do two tasks at once. When students try multitasking while doing schoolwork, they are splitting their attention. The quality of their learning gets really shallow. Students remember less and have trouble linking their learning to where it can be used in life. That, and we tend to run into things while texting and moving. Walking, riding, or driving and texting don't mix well. The same goes for texting and schoolwork. To get the most out of your reading, homework, and study time, you'll need to put the phone away. Your friends may wonder where you are for an hour, but your brain and body will thank you for a lifetime.

### How To . . .
### Lose Your Cell Phone to a Teacher in 5 Steps or Less

**STEP 1**—Sneak a text message in class.

**STEP 2**—Act surprised when the teacher sees you.

**STEP 3**—Deny sending a text message.

**STEP 4**—Claim your freedom of speech rights are being violated.

**STEP 5**—Hand over your cell phone.

# TRACK THE TEACHER

Tracking your teacher does not mean identifying their footprints and trailing them through the school's habitat and into the staff lounge. That's called *stalking*. Stalking is illegal and creepy. Stalking a teacher would probably get you suspended. Tracking your teacher is legal and helps keep you on the teacher's good list. To track your teacher, simply look at them when they are talking. If they move from one side of the class to the other, you keep watching them as they go. Hence, you track their progress through the lesson they are teaching.

## Strange but True

People get paid to read body language. Experts in reading people's body language can make a living teaching their skills at seminars or working with police departments to determine by a suspect's body language whether or not they are lying.

# TRASH

"**Y**ou can't see it from *my* house." That's what some guys say when their trash can shot misses by a mile. They walk away leaving garbage behind for somebody else to clean up. Technically that's called *littering*. It's also called rude, selfish, lazy, and it's a totally rotten thing to do. What if this was their house? More specifically, what if people lobbed litter into your bedroom and just walked off. Out of sight, out of mind . . . right? No way! You would strongly refuse (not be willing) to let other people's refuse (trash) pile up for you to pick up. The same rule applies at school. Toss your trash, and when it does fall short of the can, get your own rubbish rebound and power slam those scraps.

## *Just Joking*
**Why was the cafeteria trash can so sad?**

**He just got dumped.**

# VOICE CHANGES

**P**uberty kick-starts the growth of your body, and over the next few years, you'll go through a lot of dramatic physical developments. One of the most noticeable changes is one you won't see—you'll hear it. The deepening of your voice is a really cool thing. It happens when the vocal cords in your larynx, also know as your *voice box*, lengthen and get thicker. Think about it like this. Your vocal cords are like rubber bands. When stretched out and plucked, a thicker rubber band makes a deeper sound than a skinny one does. Puberty changes the thin vocal cords' bands in your larynx into thicker cords. Along the way, your voice will crack and squeak from time to time. Each squawk is proof the process is working. Don't worry and don't get mad. Your sounding like a poked pig won't last long. To help keep your voice in check while the transition is happening, try talking at a controlled volume level. This should help, yet there are no guarantees in puberty.

## True Story

I was talking with a good friend at school when my voice went haywire. I said three words and each one sounded like it was broken in two pieces. My friend's face froze and her eyes got wide. We both thought, "What just happened?" My face turned red and we started cracking up, laughing. We didn't say anything about my voice, we just laughed. It was an awkward situation, but nobody really cared. Voice cracks are normal in middle school.

Cole

# VOICE VOLUME

**H**ere's a quick vocal lesson for beginners. Sound is measured in units of frequency called *hertz* (Hz). The hertz of a man's voice ranges between 85 and 155, while a woman's words measure between 165 and 255 Hz. The result is, men's voices sound deeper than women's. No duh, right? But wait. Check out the vocal range of the typical kid entering middle school. The pre-puberty voices of both guys and girls wave in at 250 to 300 Hz! Add this high-pitched truth to the odd fact that kids' lung pressure is 50–60% higher than adults and what do you get? The answer isn't deep. Until puberty transforms your voice, the words that come out of your face will be two or even three times higher pitched than a man's. Yet there are ways you can make your voice sound more mature. First, when in large groups, quiet down. The combined audio adrenaline of a class talking all at once can be high-pitched enough to make dogs howl and stress a teacher out to the breaking point of assigning extra homework. Second, when you are called on in class, speak up. The class needs to hear your answer, and when you speak clearly and calmly, your voice is less likely to rise, crack, or sound flustered. In other words, your hertz will sound more mature.

## True OR False

### The smallest bone in the human body is located in your ear.

**True.** The stapes is the smallest of three tiny bones in the middle ear that convey sound from the outer ear to the inner ear.

Volume

Volume

# WRITING PAPERS

**H**andwritten or typed out, every good paper is drafted in steps.

**STEP 1**—Choose the topic. If the teacher assigns you the topic, then that step was easy.

**STEP 2**—Research information. This can be done online or in those ancient texts known as books. Either way, use only credible sources that are fact, not fan fiction.

**STEP 3**—Draft an outline. What are the general ideas you want the beginning, middle, and end of your paper to say? How many points will you make along the way?

**STEP 4**—Organize your notes. You'll need information and notes on each of your main points.

**STEP 5**—Write a first draft. Don't worry about too much editing here. Just get your thoughts down in an organized way.

**STEP 6**—Edit the paper. Do your best to make sure what you are writing makes sense and flows well. Check for correct spelling and grammar.

**STEP 7**—Have somebody else edit the paper. Be open to suggestions and willing to make any needed changes.

**STEP 8**—Prepare the final work. Format your paper exactly as the teacher assigned, and be sure to put your name on the top of the first page. Staple or bind the work as instructed, and hand that thing in, on time. Nice job, man.

## Pop Quiz

**Q:** Which animal can run the fastest: an elephant, a squirrel, or a mouse?

**A:** An elephant. Elephants can run up to 25 miles per hour.

# YEARBOOK

Captured forever on high-gloss paper, yearbooks are lasting proof of the best and many of the most embarrassing moments of middle school. Between the pictures of kids having fun, sports, clubs, and every student's picture, your friends can sign and write their own thoughts. Here are a few of the least creative yet most common comments.

"Have a great summer." "Stay cool!" "Don't ever change." "Glad I got to know you." "Hope to see you next year." "Text me sometime."

Then there are the kids who put a little effort into what they write in their friends' yearbooks. Check out these original comments:

"If you like water, then you already like over 60% of me." "If crazy people could fly, our school would be an airport." "I love it when I start laughing and you start laughing at me so hard you gasp for breath. You should know most of the time I'm laughing it's because I just passed gas." "Any size pizza is a personal pizza, if you believe in yourself." "I waited 1,095 days to write this in your yearbook. Hi."

Write what you like, just remember people tend to keep yearbooks for the rest of their lives. Go ahead and get one, write in your friends', and feel free to laugh in the future at what everybody wrote, gas or not.

## To Do in Middle School:

✓ Buy a yearbook.

# ZOMBIES

**B**elieved to be reanimated corpses capable of moving about in herds or in solo pursuit of brains to consume, zombies are feared by apocalypse preppers worldwide. The truth is, such beings are purely science fiction, unless you count some middle school students. Just watch the door of the school prior to first bell. There you will see students streaming in with glazed looks on their faces, hair matted, legs dragging, and drool spilling from their mouths. They are zombies! Or are they? Perhaps a logical explanation for their mindless herd-like movements is a lack of sleep, poor nutrition, and the belief that the day holds no real value. So how do you combat such a virus?

The antidote to zombieness is not as rare as you may think. To protect yourself, follow this three-part zombie-vanquishing plan and spread the word to anyone who will listen. First, get 8+ hours of sleep every night. Second, eat a good breakfast every morning. Third, look for something new and cool to discover and develop in yourself every day. That's it. Zombies are not real, yet students who live nearly numb lives are. Think of it this way: If you're not learning, you're not living. So go make the best of everything, and be sure to fill your middle school brain with good stuff. This time of life only comes once, so make the most of each and every day.

## Looking Back

If I could meet myself back in 1987, when I was in middle school, I'd share this one piece of advice with myself: "Be strong, brave, and of great courage! You are made of mettle!" Go ahead and look up the definition of the word *mettle*. You'll like what you find. Name it and claim it for yourself as you work your way to and through middle school. You'll be a stronger young man in the making by the time you head to high school.

Jonathan

# RIDDLE ME THIS

**1. A rooster sitting on the peak of a barn roof lays an egg. The peak of the barn roof faces north and south. It is the longest day of the year and the sun is directly overhead. Which way will the egg roll?**

**2. What do you fill with empty hands?**

**3. What has one foot on the right, one on the left, and one in the middle?**

**4. What comes once in a minute, twice in a moment, and never in a thousand years?**

**5. Two fathers and their two sons go fishing together. They each catch one fish to take home with them. They do not lose any fish, and yet when they arrive at home they only have three fish. How can this be?**

1. Roosters don't lay eggs  2. Gloves  3. A yardstick  4. The letter "M"  5. There are just three people: a grandfather, his son, and his grandson.

6. You're a bus driver. At the first stop 4 people get on. At the second stop 8 people get on. At the third stop 2 people get off, and at the fourth stop everyone got off. The question is what color are the bus driver's eyes?

7. A cowboy rode into a small western town on Friday. He stayed two nights and left on Friday. How could that be?

You'll need a calculator for the next two:

8. Think of a number.
   Key it into the calculator.
   Double it.
   Add ten.
   Halve it.
   Subtract the number you started with.
   What number are you left with?

9. Key in the first 3 numbers of your phone number. (NOT your area code.)
   Multiply by 80.
   Add 1.
   Multiply by 250.
   Add the last 4 digits of your phone number.
   Add the last 4 digits of your phone number again.
   Subtract 250.
   Divide the number by 2.
   Recognize the number?

6. The same as yours, you're the bus driver. 7. His horse's name is Friday. 8. 5 9. It's your phone number

10. How much dirt is in a hole that's 4 feet wide, 4 feet long, and 4 feet deep?

11. Anthony's mom has four children. Her first child is a girl named April. Her second child is a girl named May. Her third child is also a girl and her name is June. What is the name of her fourth child?

12. Forwards I am heavy. Backwards I am not. What am I?

13. What has hands but no feet, a face but no eyes, tells but does not talk?

14. Can you name three consecutive days without using the words Monday, Tuesday, Wednesday, Thursday, Friday, Saturday, or Sunday?

15. I am as light as a feather, yet no man can hold me for long. What am I?

16. I never was. I am always to be. No one has ever seen me, nor ever will. Yet, all expect me. What am I?

10. None. There is no dirt IN a hole. All the dirt has been removed. The calculator was only a distraction. 11. Anthony 12. Ton 13. A clock 14. Yesterday, today, tomorrow 15. Breath 16. Tomorrow

17. I have keys but no locks. I have space but no room. I can enter, but can't leave. What am I?

18. What belongs to you but others use it more often than you do?

19. What goes up and down stairs without moving?

20. I travel all around the world but never leave the corner. What am I?

21. Many have heard me, but no one has seen me, and I will not speak back until spoken to. What am I?

22. A window cleaner is cleaning a window on the top floor of a 25-floor skyscraper when, suddenly, he slips and falls! He has no safety equipment and nothing to soften his fall, yet he is not hurt. How can this be?

23. What superhero is the best baseball player?

24. What building in New York City has the most stories?

17. A keyboard 18. Your name 19. A rug 20. A stamp 21. An echo 22. He is cleaning the inside of the window. 23. Batman 24. The Library

25. Mr. and Mrs. Smith have seven daughters. If each daughter has a brother, how many children do Mr. and Mrs. Smith have?

26. What is a seven-letter word containing thousands of letters?

27. What has a head, a tail, is brown, and has no legs?

28. I'm tall when I'm young and short when I'm old. What am I?

29. What body part is pronounced as one letter but written with three, and only two different letters are used?

30. Penny has 5 children. The first is named January. The second kid is February. Her third is called March, the fourth is April. What is the name of the fifth?

31. Spell "Ghost" out loud. Then spell "Most" out loud. Then spell "Roast" out loud. What do you put in a toaster?

32. I know a word; six letters it contains. And yet if you take one away, twelve is what remains.

25. Eight. 26. Mailbox 27. A penny 28. A candle 29. Eye 30. What 31. Bread. Most people will answer "Toast." 32. Dozen(s)

**33. Which vehicle is spelled the same forwards and backwards?**

**34. When you write this time of day in capital letters, it is the same forwards, backwards, and upside down. What time is it?**

**35. What word looks the same upside down and backwards?**

This is a trick question you will have to ask to somebody else, because it only works when said out loud:

**Ask, "There are six teacups on a table. If one falls off, how many are left on the table?"**

**Answer: Five. (They will say 59, because they heard you say, "60 cups." But you actually said, "Six teacups.")**

# NOTES

1. "His Feet in 'American Idol,' and Reaching to Be a Star," *New York Times*, Jan. 11, 2004, http://www.nytimes.com/2004/01/11/arts/music-his-feet-in-american-idol-and-reaching-to-be-a-star.html.

2. Edward Schor, ed., *Caring for Your School-Age Child: Ages 5 to 12*, American Academy of Pediatrics (New York: Bantam, 2004).

3. Jonathan Catherman, *The Manual to Manhood* (Grand Rapids: Revell, 2014), 100.

4. Brian Handwerk, "Crocodiles Really Shed Tears While Eating, Study Says," *National Geographic*, Oct. 10, 2007, http://news.nationalgeographic.com/news/2007/10/071010-crocodile-tears.html.

5. Sameer Hinduja and Justin W. Patchin, *State Cyberbullying Laws*, Cyberbullying Research Center, Cyberbullying.org, updated Jan. 2016, http://cyberbullying.org/Bullying-and-Cyberbullying-Laws.pdf.

6. Jeff Kinney, *Diary of a Wimpy Kid* (New York: Amulet Books, 2007), 4.

7. http://www.brainyquote.com/quotes/authors/c/chuck_norris.html.

8. Attributed to Abraham Lincoln, http://www.azquotes.com/quote/351590.

9. Hyman G. Rickover, "The World of the Uneducated," *Saturday Evening Post*, Nov. 28, 1959, 19. 59.

10. "Secrets of Human Hair Unlocked at the Natural History Museum in London," *The Guardian*, https://www.theguardian.com/uk/2004/may/27/sciencenews.research.

11. Leah Ginnivan, "The Dirty History of Doctors' Hands," Method, http://www.methodquarterly.com/2014/11/handwashing/.

12. Daily News Staff Writers, United Press International, Feb. 18, 2009, 9:24 a.m.

13. "Longest Fingernails on a Pair of Hands (Male)—Ever," Guinness World Records, www.guinnessworldrecords.com/world-records/longest-fingernails-(male)-ever.

14. Billy Graham, quoted in J. Otis Ledbetter and Kurt D. Bruner, *Your Heritage: How to Be Intentional about the Legacy You Leave* (Chicago: Moody, 1996), 111.

15. John Medina, *Brain Rules* (Seattle, WA: Pear Press, 2008), 2.

16. Emily Graham, "Principals Do the Darndest Things," PTO Today, http://www.ptotoday.com/pto-today-articles/article/614.

17. Harry S. Truman Quotes, http://www.truman.edu/about/history/our-namesake/truman-quotes/.

18. Wikipedia contributors, "Soap," Wikipedia, https://en.wikipedia.org/w/index.php?title=Soap&oldid=764636537 (accessed February 11, 2017).

19. Jeffrey Kluger, "The New Science of Siblings," *Time*, July 10, 2006, http://content.time.com/time/magazine/article/0,9171,1209949-2,00.html.

20. "Mirror Twins: Fascinating Facts about Mirror Image Twins," Twin Pregnancy and Beyond, http://www.twin-pregnancy-and-beyond.com/mirror-twins.html.

21. "Sleep in Adolescents (13–18 Years Old)," Nationwide Children's, http://www.nationwidechildrens.org/sleep-in-adolescents.

22. "Fact Sheet: Media Use Profiles; The Common Sense Census: Media Use by Tweens and Teens," Common Sense Media, 2015, https://www.commonsensemedia.org/sites/default/files/uploads/pdfs/census_factsheet_mediauseprofiles.pdf.

23. A. Weinstein and M. Lejoyeux, "Internet Addiction or Excessive Internet Use," *American Journal of Drug and Alcohol Abuse* 36, no. 5 (Aug. 2010): 277–83.

24. "History," Olympic.org, https://www.olympic.org/ancient-olympic-games/history.

25. E. A. Kramár et al, "Synaptic Evidence for the Efficacy of Spaced Learning," NCBI, Proceedings of the National Academy of Sciences of the United States of America, 109 no. 13 (March 2012):1091–6490.

26. W. E. Hockley, "The Effects of Environmental Context on Recognition Memory and Claims of Remembering," *Journal of Experimental Psychology. Learning, Memory, and Cognition* 34 no. 6 (Feb. 2009): 278–7393.

27. Henriette van Praag, "Exercise and the Brain: Something to Chew On," *Trends in Neuroscience* 32 no. 5 (2009): 283–90.

28. Fred R. Shapiro, "Abraham Lincoln," *The Yale Book of Quotations* (New Haven: Yale University Press, 2006), 466.

29. John Wooden, "The Difference between Winning and Succeeding," TED, February 2001.

30. Hugh Jackman, interview with Rollo Ross, "That Awkward Moment When Hugh Jackman Remembers He Taught You at School," YouTube, https://www.youtube.com/watch?v=yj46BWpxFcA.

31. Victoria Shannon, "15 Years of Text Messages, a 'Cultural Phenomenon,'" *New York Times*, December 5, 2007, http://www.nytimes.com/2007/12/05/technology/05iht-sms.4.8603150.html.

**Jonathan Catherman** is the author of the bestselling *The Manual to Manhood* and is a leading education trainer specializing in the character and leadership development of youth. An award-winning cultural strategist, Jonathan speaks worldwide about the principles and strengths that empower greatness in children, teens, and young adults. As both a parent and a professional, Jonathan is committed to assisting young men in the making to experience success and significance as they mature into manhood and lifelong leadership.

Having survived middle school, **Reed Catherman** is a musician and aspiring stage performer who is committed to earning good grades, building quality relationships, and developing his talents.

As a middle school student, **Cole Catherman** is an explorer, Boy Scout, and ambitious young engineer who brings fresh insight into the concerns and questions guys have about moving up to middle school.

The Cathermans live in North Carolina. Learn more at www.jonathan catherman.com.

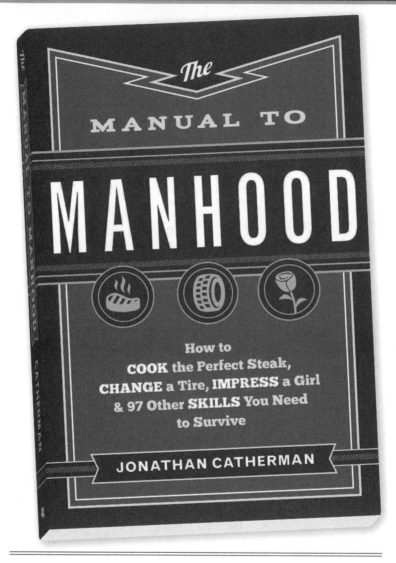